The Ultimate Meal Prep Instant Pot Cookbook for Beginners

Your Essential Guide to save time and Weight Loss – Easy, Delicious and Healthy Meals to Cook, Prep, Grab and Go

Pamel Duncan

Table of contents

CHAPTER 1: WHAT IS MEAL PREPPING?

Meal prepping in simple words is actually preparing your entire or a few meals and foods beforehand. In other words, it is just like you are having those fancy TV recipes that you are going buy from the store, except for the fact that you will be preparing them yourself, with much healthier, unprocessed and better ingredients.

It is not only time saving (which is what everyone wants these days due to their busy lifestyles), but it assists in ensuring the fact that you are consuming proper and healthier food in the right amount time to time instead of opting for canned, packaged and processed foods which are having harmful ingredients and are high in calories.

The main agenda behind this whole 'meal prepping' operation is that when you already have healthy cooked food, you won't find a reason to opt for foods which are having harmful ingredients, and this idea actually works!

How to Get Started?

This should be strictly kept in mind that you should not overwhelm yourself with different ideas in the beginner stage. It is a common phenomenon that mostly people are too caught up in every detail while they can do really good by just following the basic guidelines.

Never try introducing and then accomplishing too much innovative steps altogether. For example, never ever opt for meal prepping with recipes you haven't prepared previously. Always initiate with prepping those recipes which you know well and then with the pace of tie, depending upon your comfort level, opt for fresh recipes. Meal prepping requires doing small from to time and that is how it can be successfully applied in life. For an effective meal prepping plan, following steps should be noted and followed:

1. Select a Day:
    The very first thing is that you should accomplish is to select a day for preparing your foods. Generally, the best day for preparing your meals is Sunday, as it is a holiday so one can also take help from other family members in preparing the food and it will be very time saving as compared to working days.

    Almost every experienced meal preppers usually selects both Sunday and Wednesday to prepare their foods, this helps them dividing the foods prepping in two days for every half of the week. In the initial stages, almost nobody opts for preparing foods for the whole week;

rather they focus on 2-3 meals in the beginning. Using a simple calendar for meal prepping will benefit a lot in practically applying the meal prepping plan.

2. Select the Meals:

    It is critical to decide which meal you want to prepare first. In case of having a family, preparing the dinner will be your first priority while if you are single, lunch and breakfast will be on top of your priority list for meal prepping. After this, the next task will be selecting the recipes you want to prepare. The recipes should be balancing in their ingredients and for this you can use a kitchen scale.

3. Use Appropriate Jars & Containers:

    Perfect and proper storage containers are literally the very foundation of the whole meal prepping process. The method of how do you store your prepared food really effects meal prepping a lot. For beginners, opt for air tight jars and containers which are having air tight compartments, this single aspect will keep your food fresh, crispy and better than having it stored in a normal container. Following is the list of the most suitable and proper containers:

    - Freezer Safe
    - Microwaveable
    - Reusable
    - BPA Free
    - Dishwasher Safe
    - Stackable

What to Do in the Kitchen?

As stated earlier, always start with small and fewer meals. It is not recommended to opt for preparing meal for the entire week in the beginning. You may do it later, once you are having full command and confidence over yourself, but till then, start building your stamina for food prepping. Always start from doing small and then gradually go for the hardest meals keeping in view your capabilities and capacity.

When it comes to being in the kitchen for food prepping, following things are necessary to be followed and kept in mind for better and effective execution of the plan:

1. Aim on prepping simpler meals:

    The main agenda while food prepping is to ensure preparing simpler recipes. The reason for 'chicken' being the favorite among notably experienced meal preppers is that it can be prepared in an infinite number of methods while it is really convenient to freeze and store. Just by using chicken and some veggies, one can easily prepare 2-3 entirely different meals.

2. **Be a good multitasker:**
    You can cook different meals at one without wasting much time. Utilize your oven space at its full, either use different oven trays or go for aluminum foiling to create divisions on a single tray and prepare different meals together. Try preferring recipes which can be prepared in this manner. Whenever planning the very first shopping trip for your food prepping, do consider if you have sufficient utensils, aluminum foils and oven trays etc.

3. **Fruits:**
    Fruits are one of the most beneficial and integral part of food prepping. They can be easily cut into different sizes and stored just like any other meals that you can prepare. They can be used for preparing smoothies and fruit-salads which can be used alongside the prepped meals or even you can initiate with having only fruits as prepped meals.

4. **The Instant Pot:**
    This is the most important and critical portion of the entire food prepping plan but usually many people ignore it. The Instant Pot has taken the world by storm due to its convenience and easy cooking methods. It is very time saving and is without a doubt the best option for food preppers. Use it at its full and prepare one of the most delicious and healthy meals within no time and then store them as you like.

CHAPTER 2: WHAT ARE THE BENEFITS OF MEAL PREPPING?

There are numerous benefits of meal prepping including better nutrition and regulated metabolism. Some of them are as detailed as follows:

1. Time Saving

   It is very time saving to prepare meals for an entire week than cooking every single day. Meal prepping knocks off wasting time on cooking every day or even the time wasted in waiting for getting services at a diner or a restaurant.

2. Financially Feasible & Money Saving

   One of the most attractive advantages of meal prepping is that it is very beneficial economically. Eating at restaurants is very expensive as compared to cooking your own food at an average. The recipes in this cook book cost very low as compared to having expensive meals at restaurants and diners. If you try calculating the amount of money you spend on eating out and compare it to expenditure on cooking at home, you will clearly find the difference.

3. Keeps you focused on healthy a diet

   If you have prepared healthy food for the entire week beforehand, it is without a doubt a noted fact that you will be less likely to opt for foods and snacks having harmful ingredients in them over the food you cooked at home. This will not only help you financially but also keep your health sound and perfect.

4. Regulated Metabolism

   Whenever you feel hungry, you will be having already prepared food and thus resulting in your metabolism getting stronger. Consuming snacks on regular intervals will avoid your body getting into a catabolic state. This will stop you from having loss of lean body tissues which also includes muscles and improve your metabolism.

There are a few disadvantages of food prepping too alongside its numerous benefits. A few of them are explained as follows:

1. Lesser variety

   There is a chance that you might be eating the same food every for the whole week which is highly dependent on your meal prepping plan. It can be overcome by using different food items.

2. Time Demanding

It surely saves time but also requires time for preparing meal and the cleanup for an entire week. With time, the prepping time decreases and one can also select more than a single day for meal prepping.

CHAPTER 3: THE BASICS OF MEAL PLANNING

Meal planning or in other words 'menu planning' is the basis of meal prepping. Instead of getting worried every day for what to have for the next meal, one can easily plan his meal plan and then prepare them beforehand. It is very time and money saving alongside it ensures that you eat healthy, nutritious and a balanced diet depending on your body needs.

What differentiates Meal Prepping and Meal Planning?

Both, meal prep and meal planning work synchronously to serve a single purpose, giving you food that is healthy and nutritious in a convenient way. Meal planning is the procedure which ponders and answers the question 'what is for the next meal?' by selecting recipes as per your needs and requirements. Meal prepping on the other hand is a step in the meal planning procedure. It is basically putting all you're planning into action and executing the plan by gathering all the required ingredients for the recipes you want to prepare for the coming days or the entire week.

Advantages of Menu Planning

There are numerous benefits of menu planning. Some of them are stated as follows:

- Health benefits
  Just by preparing your food and eating homemade food, one can s ensure guaranteed sound health if your meal planning is based on a balanced and nutritious diet.
- Financial Benefits
  Menu planning helps you understand the nature of your meals and lets you draft your shopping list in a befitting and feasible manner and avoids market visits for one or two items. It also helps in knocking off impulsive purchases.

The Basics of Menu Planning

This isn't that complicated as it is framed to be. Simply write down whatever meals and recipes you like and go for them. If you are prepping and planning for the entire family, do take suggestions and input from them while planning the menu. With so much content available online, there are numerous menu planning portals and applications available online.

For efficient and befitting menu planning, plan for an entire week at a single time. Do take into consideration the inclusion of secondary dishes alongside desserts and other entrees too. After the successful completion of menu planning, draft a shopping list of all the ingredients you will need as per your drafted menu plan. To draft an effective menu plan with a proper strategic approach, following things should be kept in mind:

- Keep in view 'Dates and Days'
  Keep a check of which days or nights will be free enough to give you time for food prepping and which days or nights will be busy enough to make you opt for reheating the already prepped food. Always draft the menu planning in accordance with your schedule ahead for the time span you want to draft the menu for.

- Always keep an eye for 'sales'
  Keep an eye for sales and discount offers in different superstores, grocery stores and markets for timely availing them. It will really help a lot in financially improving your menu plans and food prepping planning.

- Keep in mind the 'season'
  Always have knowledge about which foods will be available fresh at this time of the year. This will result in the availability of the most nutritious and balanced meal with fresh ingredients right in your plate.

- Blend different food categories
  It is recommended to keep your menu colorful and versatile by blending in different food categories, planning various meat-free meals and even interchanging meals from breakfast to lunch and dinner. You can also replace new recipes with your previously liked recipes and keep on doing this cycling of bringing in new recipes from time to time.

- Imagine your plate
  The most integral part of meal planning for any occasion is to picturize your plate efficiently. It is recommended that for each meal you plan, half of your plate should be filled with fruits and veggies, a quarter with lean proteins and the rest of the quarter with preferably whole grains.

How to Master Menu Planning?

Just like any ordinary habit, menu planning gets better and better with practice and time. As soon as you spend more time in menu planning, you will realize different strategies and methods which will make the process work for you in an easy way. To plan the menu in the most convenient way possible there are some tips explained below:

- Devise themes for days:

  To make your menu colorful and versatile, decide different foods for different days and try new recipes as you get experienced.

- Reuse Leftovers:

  Reuse leftover food in different ways you like. For example, a leftover chicken can be used in a soup or with salad on any other day.

- Recycling the plan:

  Don't just throw off the menu plan after its completion. It can be used later on entirely or a portion of it can be utilized.

- Flexibility in the menu:

  You can alter your menu plan if desired. You can easily swap between recipes without much hindrance and it can keep your menu colorful without altering its nutrition and balancing.

CHAPTER 4: COMMON MISTAKES FOR MEAL PREPPING BEGINNERS

Though meal prepping isn't that complicated, yet there are certain common mistakes committed by beginners which should be avoided while following the plan.

- Insufficient Ingredients:
  Once you have devised your menu plan, go for writing down a shopping list on the basis of the menu plan. It should be having all the ingredients which are included in the menu plan so that when it comes to prepping the food, everything is on available with you.

- Preparing too much of a meal:
  With the help of meal prep the desire to order take away food can be resisted easily. But if you are preparing too much of your favorite meal regularly, you will soon get fed up of it. Try devising a menu plan which includes food from almost every category so that it remains versatile and gives you different options for every meal.

- Insufficient containers:
  Food prepping clearly requires a lot of containers and storage jars for storing the food. There are different container qualities and designs available at supermarkets which can be utilized according to the storage space and requirements of the user. Freeze the food the way its suits your requirements. Snacks can also be frozen but they have to be snap freeze first with the aid of items like slices or bliss balls placed on a lined chopping board and then freezing them individually. They can be afterwards placed in a zip lock bag without the fear of them clumping together.

- Insufficient freezer storage:
  A lot of food is feared to be wasted when you have prepared food which is filling 30 containers and your freezer's max storage space is just 20 containers. Try freeing as much storage as you can in your freezer and alongside it some of the prepped food can be stored in the refrigerator too.

- Not giving sufficient time to meal prep:

Meal prepping requires a lot of time and is not an hour game. Give yourself sufficient time to properly shop the ingredients, unpack them, chop and cook them properly and then place them in containers in the fridge after labeling them properly.

- Forgetting to label the containers:
  In order to avoid any unwanted surprises, properly name and label the containers before storing them in the freezer. Devise a proper format having the meal name, cooking date, portion numbers etc. for your convenience. You can also add details about defrosting and heating instructions too.

CHAPTER 5: TIPS

For better and efficient meal prepping, the following tips will prove to be very beneficial and helping.

1. Master Your Multitasking Skills
   Instead of preparing different meals and foods separately, try preparing them at once. Simply put ingredients in the oven or the Instant Pot and then go for preparing the rest of the food without much worry. For microwaving and freezing, the glass snap-lid storage containers can be used due to their high safety measures.

2. Prepare 1-2 Meals Maximum
   Too much variety of food will not only confuse you but will also be very time consuming to prepare too. To avoid this, prepare one or two meals at maximum and this for sure doesn't mean that the menu should be bring at all.

3. Regularly Update List of Available Items
   Keep yourself updated about the availability of ingredients in your pantry at regular intervals. This will help you decide when to shop, what to shop and how much to shop, resulting not only in time saving but also giving you a financial check about your plan.

4. Take & Devise Strategic Shortcuts
   If you are too short ion time or too caught up in your busy schedule, there is no harm at all in going for certain beneficial and convenient things from the grocery store like precut veggies etc. This will be still very good on economic and health as compared to take away.

5. Cut-short the Recipes
   Recipes usually involve complicated and time-consuming steps, cut them short and prepare food according to your need and requirements. Try focusing on simple foods like veggies and roasted chickens, low-maintenance soups, slices veggies and boiled eggs etc.

6. Take Suggestions in the Menu
   If you are prepping for the entire family, try taking suggestions and input from the entire family before menu planning so that the entire family can have a proper food without any dominance from a single person's choices.

7. Entertain Yourself While Prepping
   Prepping doesn't require you to be silent; you can listen to audio books, podcasts and music etc. while prepping food.

CHAPTER 6: INSTANT POT BASICS

Composition

It is really hard to believe that you can have tons of functions in a single cooking device. The instant pot can be divided into three basic components namely inner pot, lid lock and the housing. The inner pot is separable and is made up of stainless steel with a sturdy bottom for cooking with uniformity. The lid lock is basically a gasket and airtight chamber insuring that the lid is sealed in the right position. As a safety power switch, the instant pot does not start heating unless the lid is the right position. If there is a lot of pressure built inside the instant pot the pin lock mechanism of its float valves makes sure that it does not open accidentally. Next comes the brain of the device which is the housing unit. It consists of sensors, the heating element and the control box. The pressure and temperature are monitored by the help of sensors. In order to control the timing and cooking cycles there is a microprocessor. Also an audible alarm is installed in case of any trouble. Power supply may also be cut off.

The keys for operation include plus, minus, adjust and pressure. Plus, minus keys deal with cooking functions including soup, meat, multigrain and other manual functions. The pressure key has no impact on non-pressure cooking functions which include the slow cooking, sauté and making yogurt.

Ratings

Instant Pot is at the top of selling brands on Amazon and has really good overall customer ratings. It has up to 1 Million highly involved consumers and its demand is growing day by day. Sharing recipes, offering tips, product suggestions and question-answer sessions is becoming easier every day. This company was founded back in 2009 by a team of Canadian veterans who want to bring their own personal experiences into cooking. The objective is to help busy families and to provide them with a device which can assist in healthy cooking. They have raised the bar by being user-friendly, providing security and multi-functionality. As the company begins to develop new products, the world waits for more assistance in cooking.

However, having said that, we must remember that instant pot may not be that quick. We might have to wait for pressure to build up inside the pot for it to actually start cooking. Some recipes may require time to make. It is preferred to buy a pot having a bigger size as we can fill it up to only 2/3 of its total size. The instant pot has stainless steel which means we don't have to worry about heavy metals affecting our food. It may be noted that although, your house may not smell like the item which is being cooked, the inner seal might have some traces.

Guidelines

- Remember the total cooking time.
- Instant pot does not need to be on the stove pot.
- Be careful while opening the lid at the end.
- There should be at least one cup of some form of liquid involved in the cooking
- If the meat is undercooked, you may give it some more time.
- Milk or thicker are not required for pressure cooking.
- Manual reading is highly recommended.
- Recipe scripts should be chosen wisely; start from easier and gradually move to the harder ones.
- Sauté function helps with browning. Both things are more or less the same.
- Pressure release options should be well understood by the user before cooking
- Try to keep your pot as clean as possible.
- Remember not to fill your pot more than two-third of its capacity.
- Recipes for traditional cooking may require amendments when cooking with this device as there is little to no evaporation involved. Quantities of liquid need to be checked. There are many recipes which are published for slow cooking and they involve already prepared seasonings and sauces.
- Because food is cooked in such a device, it stays warmer for a longer period of time and can be reused without reheating.

Instant Pot Benefits

Some of the amazing benefits of Instant Pot are explained as follows:

- **Replacement of Old Appliances**
  It is a state of the art cooking appliance which is designed to replace several appliances of our kitchens namely pressure cooker, rice cooker, slow cooker, sauté pan, food warmer and many more.

- **Bluetooth Facility**
  It comes with Bluetooth; making it technologically advanced allowing connectivity with Smartphones and tablets.

- **Healthy and Delicious Food**
  It is designed to make nutritional, tasty and quick food. It helps preserve more vitamins and minerals in natural ingredients. It helps to eliminate harmful bacteria and the pressure inside is very high reducing the risk of eaters falling sick.

- **Time Saver**
  Since this is a relatively new concept, certain chefs are gradually giving out recipes which can be used to make food using this device. Complex steps can easily be converted to recipe scripts which can then be uploaded to produce good results every time.

- **Easy to Handle**
  Instant Pot is very easy and convenient to handle. There are many sensors installed and the microprocessor can make our cooking as easy as pressing a button.

- **Energy Saver**

  It saves 70% of our energy as compared to traditional cooking methods.

- **Avoidance of Errors**
  This device also helps to avoid errors and safety hazards as compared to the common pressure cooker.

- **Multi-functional Device**

It is multifunctional meaning it helps simmering, browning, fermenting, keeping warm, making yogurt and to sauté. There are up to14 convenient cooking programs which are all controlled by a microprocessor.

- Pleasant Process
  The processor manages the time allowing us to do other things while cooking. This process is pleasant and produces much less noise. It increases the aromas and flavors of our food as well.

- Food Innovation
  It comes with dual pressure settings; fast and flexible giving us a lot of room to play around and innovating with our food.

CHAPTER 7: BREAKFAST RECIPES

Spiced Quinoa

Preparation Time: 10 minutes
Cooking Time: 12 minutes
Servings: 6
Ingredients:

- 1½ cups water
- 15-ounce unsweetened almond milk
- 1½ cups uncooked quinoa, rinsed
- ¼ cup pure maple syrup
- 1 teaspoon pure vanilla extract
- 1 teaspoon ground cinnamon
- 1/8 teaspoon ground ginger
- Pinch of ground nutmeg
- Pinch of salt
- ½ cup fresh blueberries

Method:

1. In the pot of Instant Pot, add all ingredients except blueberries and stir to combine well.
2. Secure the lid and place the pressure valve to "Seal" position.
3. Select "Rice" and just use the default time of 12 minutes.
4. Select the "Cancel" and carefully do a "Natural" release for about 10 minutes and then do a "Quick" release.
5. Remove the lid and with a fork, fluff the quinoa.
6. Serve with the topping of blueberries.

Meal Prep Tip: Transfer the cooked quinoa mixture into 6 jars and keep aside to cool. Cover tightly with a lid and refrigerate for 1-2 days. Reheat in microwave before serving. Top with blueberries and serve.

Nutritional Value per Serving:

- Calories 212
- Total Fat 3.7 g
- Saturated Fat 0.4 g
- Cholesterol 0 mg
- Sodium 82 mg
- Total Carbs 38.9 g

- *Fiber 3.8 g*
- *Sugar 9.1 g*
- *Protein 6.4 g*
- *Potassium 333 mg*

Pumpkin Oatmeal

Preparation Time: 10 minutes

Cooking Time: 3 minutes

Servings: 8

Ingredients:

- 4½ cups water
- 1½ cups steel-cut oats
- 1½ cups pumpkin puree
- 2 teaspoons ground cinnamon
- 1 teaspoon ground allspice
- 1 teaspoon vanilla extract
- ½ cup brown sugar
- ¼ cup almonds, chopped

Method:

1. In the pot of Instant Pot, add all ingredients except brown sugar and almonds and stir to combine.
2. Secure the lid and place the pressure valve to "Seal" position.
3. Select "Manual" and cook under "Manual" and "High Pressure" for about 3 minutes.
4. Select the "Cancel" and carefully do a "Natural" release.
5. Remove the lid and stir in brown sugar until well combined.
6. Top with almonds and serve.

Meal Prep Tip: Transfer the oatmeal into 8 small jars and keep aside to cool. Cover tightly with a lid and refrigerate for 1 day.

Nutritional Value per Serving:

- *Calories 198*
- *Total Fat 3.9 g*
- *Saturated Fat 0.6 g*
- *Cholesterol 0 mg*
- *Sodium 5 mg*
- *Total Carbs 35.7 g*
- *Fiber 5.8 g*
- *Sugar 10.5 g*
- *Protein 6.4 g*
- *Potassium 134 mg*

Amaranth Porridge

Preparation Time: 10 minutes

Cooking Time: 3 minutes

Servings: 4

Ingredients:

- 2½ cups unsweetened almond milk
- 1 cup uncooked amaranth
- 2 ripe bananas, peeled and sliced
- ½ teaspoon ground cinnamon

Method:

1. In the pot of Instant Pot, mix together all ingredients.
2. Secure the lid and place the pressure valve to "Seal" position.
3. Select "Manual" and cook under "Manual" and "High Pressure" for about 3 minutes.
4. Select the "Cancel" and carefully do a "Natural" release.
5. Remove the lid and stir the mixture well.
6. Serve warm.

Meal Prep Tip: Transfer the porridge into 8 small jars and keep aside to cool. Cover tightly with a lid and refrigerate for 1 day.

Nutritional Value per Serving:

- *Calories 261*
- *Total Fat 5.6 g*
- *Saturated Fat 1.1 g*
- *Cholesterol 0 mg*
- *Sodium 123 mg*
- *Total Carbs 47.2 g*
- *Fiber 6.8 g*
- *Sugar 8.1 g*
- *Protein 8.3 g*
- *Potassium 510 mg*

Cornmeal Porridge

Preparation Time: 10 minutes

Cooking Time: 6 minutes

Servings: 4

Ingredients:

- 1 cup fine yellow cornmeal
- 4 cups water, divided
- 1 cup milk
- 2 cinnamon sticks
- 3 pimento berries
- 1 teaspoon vanilla extract
- ½ teaspoon ground nutmeg
- ½ cup sweetened condensed milk

Method:

1. In a bowl, add cornmeal and 1 cup of water and beat until well combined.
2. In the pot of Instant Pot, place remaining ingredients except the condensed milk and stir to combine.
3. Add cornmeal mixture and stir to combine.
4. Secure the lid and place the pressure valve to "Seal" position.
5. Select "Porridge" and just use the default time of 6 minutes.
6. Select the "Cancel" and carefully do a "Natural" release.
7. Remove the lid and stir in the condensed milk.
8. Serve immediately.

Meal Prep Tip: Transfer the porridge into 4 jars and keep aside to cool. Cover tightly with a lid and refrigerate for 1-2 days. Reheat in microwave before serving.

Nutritional Value per Serving:

- *Calories 268*
- *Total Fat 5.8 g*
- *Saturated Fat 3.1 g*
- *Cholesterol 18 mg*
- *Sodium 95 mg*
- *Total Carbs 47.5 g*
- *Fiber 2.3 g*
- *Sugar 24 g*
- *Protein 7.5 g*

Scallion Omelet

Preparation Time: 10 minutes

Cooking Time: 5 minutes

Serving: 1

Ingredients:

- 1 large egg
- 1/3 cup water
- Pinch of garlic powder
- Salt and freshly ground black pepper, to taste
- 1 scallion, chopped
- Pinch of sesame seeds

Method:

1. Arrange a steamer trivet in the bottom of Instant Pot and pour 1 cup of water.
2. In a heatproof bowl, add egg, water, garlic powder, salt and black pepper and beat until well combined.
3. Stir in scallion and sesame seeds.
4. Place the bowl on top of trivet.
5. Secure the lid and place the pressure valve to "Seal" position.
6. Select "Manual" and cook under "Manual" and "High Pressure" for about 5 minutes.
7. Select the "Cancel" and carefully do a "Quick" release.
8. Remove the lid and serve immediately.

Meal Prep Tip: Transfer the omelet onto a plate and keep aside to cool completely. In a resealable plastic bag, place the cooled omelet and seal the bag. Refrigerate for about 2-4 days. Reheat in the microwave on High for about 1 minute before serving.

Nutritional Value per Serving:

- Calories 80
- Total Fat 5.2 g
- Saturated Fat 1.6 g
- Cholesterol 186 mg
- Sodium 230 mg
- Total Carbs 1.8 g
- Fiber 0.5 g
- Sugar 0.8 g
- Protein 6.7 g

Milky Pancakes

Preparation Time: 15 minutes
Cooking Time: 45 minutes
Servings: 5

Ingredients:

- 2 cups all-purpose flour
- 2½ teaspoons baking powder
- 2 tablespoons granulated white sugar
- 1½ cups milk
- 2 large eggs
- 2 tablespoons unsweetened applesauce

Method:

1. In a bowl, mix together flour, baking powder and sugar.
2. In another bowl, add milk and eggs and beat until well combined.
3. Add flour mixture and mix until smooth.
4. Generously, grease the pot of Instant Pot.
5. Place the flour mixture into prepared Instant Pot.
6. Secure the lid and place the pressure valve to "Seal" position.
7. Select "Manual" and cook under "High Pressure" for about 45 minutes.
8. Select the "Cancel" and carefully do a "Natural" release.
9. Remove the lid and carefully, pop the mixture out upside down so that the bottom is now the top.
10. Cut into 5 equal sized wedges and serve with the drizzling of applesauce.

Meal Prep Tip: Keep the pancake wedges aside to cool completely. Place a layer of wax paper between each pancake wedge. In a resealable plastic bag, place the pancake stack and seal the bag. Refrigerate for about 1-2 days. Reheat in the microwave on Medium for about 2 minutes before serving.

Nutritional Value per Serving:

- Calories 267
- Total Fat 3.8 g
- Cholesterol 71 mg
- Sodium 63 mg
- Fiber 1.5 g
- Protein 9.8 g
- Potassium 376 mg

Banana Bread

Preparation Time: 15 minutes
Cooking Time: 50 minutes
Servings: 10
Ingredients:

- 2 cups flour
- 1 teaspoon baking powder
- ½ cup sugar
- ½ cup butter, softened
- 2 eggs
- 1 tablespoon vanilla extract
- 4 bananas, peeled and mashed

Method:

1. Grease a 7-inch springform pan and keep aside.
2. In a bowl, mix together flour and baking powder.
3. In another bowl, add sugar, butter and eggs and beat until creamy.
4. Add bananas and vanilla extract and beat until well combined.
5. Slowly, add flour mixture, 1 cup at a time and mix until smooth.
6. Place the mixture into prepared springform pan evenly.
7. Arrange a steamer trivet in the bottom of Instant Pot. Add 1 cup of water in Instant Pot.
8. Place the springform pan on top of trivet.
9. Secure the lid and place the pressure valve to "Seal" position.
10. Select "Manual" and cook under "High Pressure" for about 50 minutes.
11. Select the "Cancel" and carefully do a "Quick" release.
12. Remove the lid and transfer the pan onto a wire rack to cool for about 10 minutes.
13. Carefully, invert bread onto wire rack to cool completely.
14. Cut into desired sized slices and serve.

Meal Prep Tip: In a resealable plastic bag, place the cooled bread slices and seal the bag after squeezing the excess air. Keep the bread away from direct sunlight and preserve in a cool and dry place for about 1-2 days.

Nutritional Value per Serving:

- *Calories 269*
- *Cholesterol 57 mg*
- *Fiber 1.9 g*

Kale Muffins

Preparation Time: 15 minutes

Cooking Time: 6 minutes

Servings: 6

Ingredients:

- 8 large eggs
- ¼ cup milk
- ¼ teaspoon red pepper flakes, crushed
- Salt and freshly ground black pepper, to taste
- 1 cup fresh kale, trimmed and chopped
- ½ cup tomato, seeded and chopped
- 2 scallions, sliced
- 1/3 cup Parmesan cheese, shredded

Method:

1. Grease 6 (6-ounce) ovenproof custard cups.
2. In a large bowl, add the eggs, milk, red pepper flakes, salt and black pepper and beat until well combined.
3. In another bowl, mix together the vegetables.
4. Divide the vegetable mixture into prepared custard cups evenly and top with egg mixture, followed by the Parmesan cheese.
5. Arrange a steamer trivet in the bottom of Instant Pot and pour 1 cup of water.
6. Place 3 custard cups on top of the trivet.
7. Now, arrange a second trivet on top of custard cups.
8. Place the remaining custard cups on top of second trivet.
9. Secure the lid and place the pressure valve to "Seal" position.
10. Select "Manual" and cook under "High Pressure" for about 6 minutes.
11. Select the "Cancel" and carefully do a "Natural" release for about 5 minutes and then do a "Quick" release.
12. Remove the lid and keep onto a wire rack to cool for about 10 minutes.
13. Carefully invert the muffins onto serving plates and serve warm.

Meal Prep Tip: Carefully invert the muffins onto a wire rack to cool completely. Line 1-2 airtight container with paper towels. Arrange muffins over paper towel in a single layer. Cover muffins with another paper towel. Refrigerate for about 2-3 days. Reheat in the microwave on High for about 2 minutes before serving.

Nutritional Value per Serving:

- *Calories 166*
- *Total Fat 10.5 g*
- *Saturated Fat 4.5 g*
- *Cholesterol 358 mg*
- *Sodium 126 mg*
- *Total Carbs 3.6 g*
- *Fiber 0.5 g*
- *Sugar 1.5 g*
- *Protein 14.3 g*
- *Potassium 214 mg*

CHAPTER 8: FISH AND SEAFOOD

Citrus Salmon

Preparation Time: 15 minutes
Cooking Time: 7 minutes
Servings: 4

Ingredients:

- 4 (4-ounce) salmon fillets
- 1 teaspoon fresh ginger, minced
- 2 teaspoons fresh orange zest, grated finely
- 1 cup white wine
- 1 tablespoon olive oil
- 3 tablespoons fresh orange juice
- Salt and freshly ground black pepper, to taste

Method:

1. In the pot of Instant Pot, add all ingredients and gently, stir to combine.
2. Secure the lid and place the pressure valve to "Seal" position.
3. Secure the lid and place the pressure valve to "Seal" position.
4. Select "Manual" and cook under "High Pressure" for about 7 minutes.
5. Select the "Cancel" and carefully do a "Natural" release.
6. Remove the lid and transfer the salmon fillets onto serving plates.
7. Top with the cooking sauce and serve.

Meal Prep Tip: Transfer the salmon fillets onto a platter and keep aside to cool completely. Divide the salmon fillets into 4 containers evenly ant top each with cooking sauce. Cover the containers and refrigerate for 2 days. Reheat in the microwave before serving.

Nutritional Value per Serving:

- *Calories 237*
- *Total Fat 10.6 g*
- *Saturated Fat 1.5 g*
- *Cholesterol 50 mg*
- *Sodium 29 mg*
- *Total Carbs 3.4 g*
- *Fiber 0.2 g*
- *Sugar 1.5 g*
- *Protein 22.2 g*

Lemony Salmon

Preparation Time: 15 minutes

Cooking Time: 3 minutes

Servings: 4

Ingredients:

- ¼ cup extra-virgin olive oil
- 2 tablespoons fresh lemon juice
- 1 garlic clove, minced
- 1 tablespoon feta cheese, crumbled
- ¼ teaspoon dried oregano
- Salt and freshly ground black pepper, to taste
- 1-pound salmon fillets
- 4 fresh rosemary sprigs
- 4 lemon slices

Method:

1. In a large bowl, add oil, lemon juice, garlic, feta, oregano, salt and black pepper and beat until well co combined.
2. Arrange a steamer trivet in the bottom of Instant Pot and pour 1½ cups of water.
3. Place the salmon fillets on top of trivet in a single layer and top with dressing.
4. Arrange 1 rosemary sprig and 1 lemon slice over each fillet.
5. Secure the lid and place the pressure valve to "Seal" position.
6. Select "Steam" and just use the default time of 3 minutes.
7. Select the "Cancel" and carefully do a "Quick" release.
8. Remove the lid and serve hot.

Meal Prep Tip: Transfer the salmon fillets onto a platter and keep aside to cool completely. Divide the salmon fillets into 4 containers. Cover the containers and refrigerate for 2 days. Reheat in the microwave before serving.

Nutritional Value per Serving:

- *Calories 269*
- *Total Fat 20.2 g*
- *Saturated Fat 3.2 g*
- *Cholesterol 52 mg*
- *Total Carbs 1.2 g*
- *Fiber 0.3 g*
- *Sugar 0.5 g*

Sweet & Sour Mahi-Mahi

Preparation Time: 15 minutes

Cooking Time: 5 minutes

Servings: 2

Ingredients:

- 2 (4-ounce) mahi-mahi fillets
- Salt and freshly ground black pepper, to taste
- 2 garlic cloves, minced
- 2 tablespoons fresh lime juice
- 2 tablespoons honey
- 1 teaspoon red pepper flakes, crushed
- 1 tablespoon fresh parsley, chopped

Method:

1. Season the mahi-mahi fillets with salt and black pepper evenly.
2. In a bowl, mix together remaining ingredients.
3. Arrange the trivet in the bottom of Instant Pot. Add 1 cup of water in Instant Pot.
4. Place the fish fillets on top of trivet in a single layer and top with sauce.
5. Secure the lid and place the pressure valve to "Seal" position.
6. Select "Steam" and just use the default time of 5 minutes.
7. Select the "Cancel" and carefully do a "Quick" release.
8. Remove the lid and serve hot with the garnishing of parsley.

Meal Prep Tip: Transfer the mahi-mahi fillets onto a platter and keep aside to cool completely. Divide the mahi-mahi fillets into 2 containers. Cover the containers and refrigerate for 2 days. Reheat in the microwave before serving.

Nutritional Value per Serving:

- Calories 163
- Total Fat 0.2 g
- Saturated Fat 0 g
- Cholesterol 40 mg
- Sodium 139 mg
- Total Carbs 19 g
- Fiber 0.4 g
- Sugar 17.4 g
- Protein 21.5 g
- Potassium 52 mg

Mahi-Mahi in Tomato Sauce

Preparation Time: 15 minutes
Cooking Time: 14 minutes
Servings: 6
Ingredients:

- 2 tablespoons butter
- 1 (28-ounce) can diced tomatoes
- 1 yellow onion, sliced
- 2 tablespoons fresh lemon juice
- 1 teaspoon dried oregano
- Salt and freshly ground black pepper, to taste
- 6 (4-ounce) mahi-mahi fillets

Method:

1. Place the butter in the Instant Pot and select "Sauté". Then add all ingredients except fish fillets and cook for about 8-10 minutes.
2. Select the "Cancel" and place fish fillets over sauce. With a spoon, place some sauce over fillets.
3. Secure the lid and place the pressure valve to "Seal" position.
4. Select "Manual" and cook under "High Pressure" for about 4 minutes.
5. Select the "Cancel" and carefully do a "Quick" release.
6. Remove the lid and serve hot with the topping of sauce.

Meal Prep Tip: Transfer the mahi-mahi mixture into a large bowl and keep aside to cool completely. Divide the mixture into 6 containers. Cover the containers and refrigerate for about 2 days. Reheat in the microwave before serving.

Nutritional Value per Serving:

- Calories 157
- Total Fat 4.2 g
- Saturated Fat 2.5 g
- Cholesterol 50 mg
- Sodium 158 mg
- Total Carbs 7.1g
- Fiber 2.1 g
- Sugar 4.4 g
- Protein 22.5 g
- Potassium 124 mg

Cod with Tomatoes

Preparation Time: 15 minutes

Cooking Time: 5 minutes

Servings: 4

Ingredients:

- 1-pound cherry tomatoes, halved
- 2 tablespoons fresh rosemary, chopped
- 4 (4-ounce) cod fillets
- 2 garlic cloves, minced
- 1 tablespoon olive oil
- Salt and freshly ground black pepper, to taste

Method:

1. In the bottom of a greased large heatproof bowl, place half of cherry tomatoes, followed by the rosemary.
2. Arrange cod fillets on top in a single layer, followed by the remaining tomatoes.
3. Sprinkle with garlic and drizzle with oil.
4. Arrange the bowl into Instant Pot.
5. Secure the lid and place the pressure valve to "Seal" position.
6. Select "Manual" and cook under "High Pressure" for about 5 minutes.
7. Select the "Cancel" and carefully do a "Quick" release.
8. Remove the lid and transfer the fish fillets and tomatoes in serving plates.
9. Sprinkle with salt and black pepper and serve.

Meal Prep Tip: Transfer the cooked cod mixture onto a platter and keep aside to cool completely. Divide the cod mixture into 4 containers. Cover the containers and refrigerate for 2 days. Reheat in the microwave before serving.

Nutritional Value:

- *Calories 149*
- *Total Fat 5 g*
- *Saturated Fat 0.7 g*
- *Cholesterol 56 mg*
- *Sodium 116 mg*
- *Total Carbs 6 g*
- *Fiber 2.1 g*
- *Sugar 3 g*
- *Protein 21.4 g*

Spicy Trout

Preparation Time: 10 minutes

Cooking Time: 5 minutes

Servings: 2

Ingredients:

- ½ teaspoon ground cumin
- ½ teaspoon ground coriander
- ¼ teaspoon ground turmeric
- Salt and freshly ground black pepper, to taste
- 2 (5-ounce) trout fillets

Method:

1. In a bowl, mix together spices.
2. Coat the trout fillets with the spice mixture generously.
3. In the bottom of Instant Pot, arrange a steamer trivet and pour 1 cup of water.
4. Place the trout fillets on top of trivet.
5. Secure the lid and place the pressure valve to "Seal" position.
6. Select "Steam" and just use the default time of 5 minutes.
7. Select the "Cancel" and carefully do a "Quick" release.
8. Remove the lid and serve immediately.

Meal Prep Tip: Transfer the trout fillets onto a platter and keep aside to cool completely. Divide the trout fillets into 2 containers. Cover the containers and refrigerate for 2 days. Reheat in the microwave before serving.

Nutritional Value per Serving:

- Calories 272
- Total Fat 12.2 g
- Saturated Fat 2.1 g
- Cholesterol 105 mg
- Sodium 174 mg
- Total Carbs 0.4 g
- Fiber 0.1 g
- Sugar 0 g
- Protein 37.9 g
- Potassium 673 mg

Seabass Curry

Preparation Time: 15 minutes

Cooking Time: 18 minutes

Servings: 4

Ingredients:

- 1 (14½-ounce) can coconut milk
- 1 tablespoon fresh lime juice
- 1 tablespoon red curry paste
- 2 teaspoons Sriracha
- 1 teaspoon soy sauce
- 1 teaspoon fish sauce
- 1 teaspoon honey
- 2 garlic cloves, minced
- 1 teaspoon ground ginger
- Salt and ground white pepper, to taste
- 1-pound sea bass, cut into 1-inch cubes
- ¼ cup fresh cilantro, chopped

Method:

1. In a large bowl, add all ingredients except fish and cilantro and mix until well combined.
2. In the pot of Instant Pot, place sea bass and top with coconut milk mixture evenly.
3. Secure the lid and place the pressure valve to "Seal" position.
4. Select "Manual" and cook under "High Pressure" for about 3 minutes.
5. Select the "Cancel" and carefully do a "Quick" release.
6. Remove the lid and serve hot with the garnishing of cilantro.

Meal Prep Tip: Transfer the scurry except the cilantro into a bowl and keep aside to cool completely. Divide the curry into 4 containers. Cover the containers and refrigerate for 1-2 days. Reheat in the microwave before serving. Garnish with cilantro and serve.

Nutritional Value:

- *Calories 272*
- *Total Fat 9.9 g*
- *Saturated Fat 1.5 g*
- *Cholesterol 216 mg*
- *Sodium 348 mg*
- *Total Carbs 6.3 g*
- *Fiber 1.4 g*

Shrimp Scampi

Preparation Time: 15 minutes

Cooking Time: 7 minutes

Servings: 4

Ingredients:

- 2 tablespoons salted butter
- 2 shallots, chopped
- 1 tablespoon garlic, crushed
- ¼ cup white wine
- 1 pound frozen large shrimp, peeled and deveined
- ½ cup chicken broth
- 2 tablespoons fresh lemon juice
- Salt and freshly ground black pepper, to taste
- 1 tablespoons Parmesan cheese, shredded

Method:

1. Place the butter in the Instant Pot and select "Sauté". Then add the shallots and garlic and cook for about 2-3 minutes.
2. Stir in the wine and cook for about 1 minute.
3. Select the "Cancel" and stir in shrimp, broth, lemon juice, salt and black pepper.
4. Secure the lid and place the pressure valve to "Seal" position.
5. Select "Manual" and cook under "High Pressure" for about 3 minutes.
6. Select the "Cancel" and carefully do a "Quick" release.
7. Remove the lid and
8. Close the Power Pressure Cooker by locking the lid and set the "Valve" to pressure cooking position.
9. Select "Manual" and cook under "High Pressure" for about 1 minute.
10. Select the "Cancel" and carefully do a Quick release.
11. Remove the lid and serve hot with the topping of cheese.

Meal Prep Tip: Transfer the cooked shrimp mixture into a bowl and keep aside to cool completely. Divide the shrimp mixture into 4 containers. Cover the containers and refrigerate for 1-2 days. Reheat in the microwave before serving.

Nutritional Value:

- *Calories 219*
- *Total Fat 8.3 g*
- *Saturated Fat 4.6 g*

Seafood Stew

Preparation Time: 15 minutes
Cooking Time: 15 minutes
Servings: 4

Ingredients:

- 3 tablespoons olive oil
- 2 teaspoons paprika
- 2 bay leaves
- 1½ cups tomatoes, chopped
- 1 small green bell pepper, seeded and sliced thinly
- 1 small onion, sliced thinly
- 2 garlic cloves, minced
- 1 cup fish broth
- Salt and freshly ground black pepper, to taste
- 1-pound shrimp, peeled and deveined
- 12 Little neck clams
- 1½ pounds cod fillets, cut into 2-inch chunks
- ¼ cup fresh cilantro, chopped

Method:

1. Place the oil in the Instant Pot and select "Sauté". Then add the paprika and bay leaves and cook for about 15-20 seconds.
2. Add the tomatoes, bell pepper, onion and garlic and cook for about 3-4 minutes.
3. Select the "Cancel" and stir in broth, salt and black pepper.
4. Place the shrimp and clams on top and gently, submerge in broth mixture. Arrange cod pieces on top.
5. Secure the lid and place the pressure valve to "Seal" position.
6. Select "Manual" and cook under "High Pressure" for about 10 minutes.
7. Select the "Cancel" and carefully do a Natural release for about 10 minutes and then do a Quick release.
8. Remove the lid and serve hot with the garnishing of cilantro.

Meal Prep Tip: Transfer the stew except the cilantro into a bowl and keep aside to cool completely. Divide the stew into 6 containers. Cover the containers and refrigerate for 1-2 days. Reheat in the microwave before serving. Garnish with cilantro and serve.

Nutritional Value:

- *Calories 272*

- Total Fat 9.9 g
- Saturated Fat 1.5 g
- Cholesterol 216 mg
- Sodium 348 mg
- Total Carbs 6.3 g
- Fiber 1.4 g
- Sugar 2.8 g
- Protein 39.6 g
- Potassium 377 mg

CHAPTER 9: SNACK RECIPES

Candied Lemon Peel

Preparation Time: 15 minutes

Cooking Time: 20 minutes

Servings: 50

Ingredients:

- 1 pound lemons
- 5 cups water, divided
- 2¼ cups white sugar, divided

Method:

1. Slice the lemon in half lengthwise and extract juice. Discard the juice.
2. Slice each half in quarters and with a melon-baller, remove the pulp.
3. Cut the lemon quarters into thin strips.
4. In the pot Instant Pot, place lemon peel strips and 4 cups of water.
5. Secure the lid and place the pressure valve to "Seal" position.
6. Select "Manual" and cook under "High Pressure" for about 3 minutes.
7. Select the "Cancel" and carefully do a Natural release.
8. Remove the lid and strain the lemon peel strips.
9. Rinse the strips completely.
10. Remove water from the pot and with paper towels, pat dry it.
11. Place the lemon peel strips, 2 cups of sugar and remaining 1 cup of water in the Instant Pot and select "Sauté".
12. Cook for about 5 minutes.
13. Select the "Cancel".
14. Secure the lid and place the pressure valve to "Seal" position.
15. Select "Manual" and cook under "High Pressure" for about 10 minutes.
16. Select the "Cancel" and carefully do a "Natural" release.
17. Remove the lid and strain the peel strips.
18. Spread the peel strips onto a cutting board for about 15-20 minutes.
19. In a shallow bowl, place remaining sugar
20. Coat lemon strips with sugar, shaking off the excess.
21. Arrange lemon strips onto a sheet pan and refrigerate, uncovered for at least 4 hours or overnight.

Meal Prep Tip: Transfer the cooled lemon peel into airtight containers. Cover tightly with a lid and store for up to 7 days.

Nutritional Value per Serving:

- Calories 36
- Total Fat 0 g
- Saturated Fat 0 g
- Cholesterol 0 mg
- Sodium 1 mg
- Total Carbs 9.9 g
- Fiber 0.3 g
- Sugar 9.2 g
- Protein 01 g
- Potassium 13 mg

Crunchy Walnuts

Preparation Time: 15 minutes

Cooking Time: 20 minutes

Servings: 32

Ingredients:

- 1 teaspoon butter
- 4 cups raw walnuts
- 2/3 cup maple syrup
- ½ tablespoon vanilla extract
- 2 teaspoons ground cinnamon
- ½ teaspoon ground nutmeg
- ¼ teaspoon salt
- ½ cup water

Method:

1. Select "Sauté" of Instant Pot. Add all ingredients except water and cook for about 5 minutes, stirring frequently.
2. Select the "Cancel" and stir in about ½ cup of water.
3. Secure the lid and place the pressure valve to "Seal" position.
4. Select "Manual" and cook under "High Pressure" for about 10 minutes.
5. Meanwhile, preheat the oven to 350 degrees F.
6. Select the "Cancel" and carefully do a "Natural" release for about 10 minutes and then do a "Quick" release.
7. Remove the lid and transfer the walnuts onto a baking sheet.
8. Bake for about 5 minutes.
9. Remove from oven and keep aside to cool before serving.

Meal Prep Tip: Transfer the cooled walnuts into airtight containers. Cover tightly with a lid and store for up to 7 days.

Nutritional Value per Serving:

- *Calories 116*
- *Total Fat 9.4 g*
- *Saturated Fat 0.6 g*
- *Cholesterol 0 mg*
- *Sodium 21 mg*
- *Total Carbs 6.1 g*
- *Fiber 1.1 g*

Chickpeas Trail Mix

Preparation Time: 15 minutes

Cooking Time: 23 minutes

Servings: 20

Ingredients:

- 10-ounce canned chickpeas, drained
- 1½ cups raw pecan halves
- 1 cup raw almonds
- ½ cup cashews
- ¼ cup raw sunflower seeds
- 3 tablespoons butter
- ½ cup pure maple syrup
- 1 tablespoon spicy Cajun seasoning
- Pinch of ground ginger
- Pinch of salt
- 6-ounce dried mango

Method:

1. Select "Sauté" of Instant Pot. Add all ingredients and cook for about 2-3 minutes, stirring frequently.
2. Secure the lid and place the pressure valve to "Seal" position.
3. Select "Manual" and cook under "High Pressure" for about 10 minutes.
4. Meanwhile, preheat the oven to 375 degrees F.
5. Select the "Cancel" and carefully do a "Quick" release.
6. Remove the lid and transfer the mixture onto a baking sheet.
7. Bake for about 7-10 minutes, flipping once in the middle way.
8. Remove from oven and keep aside to cool completely before serving.

Meal Prep Tip: Transfer the cooled pecans into airtight containers. Cover tightly with a lid and store for up to 7 days.

Nutritional Value per Serving:

- *Calories 206*
- *Total Fat 13.3 g*
- *Saturated Fat 2.4 g*
- *Cholesterol 5 mg*
- *Sodium 32 mg*
- *Total Carbs 18.7 g*

Turkey Meatballs

Preparation Time: 15 minutes

Cooking Time: 25 minutes

Servings: 8

Ingredients:

- 1-pound lean ground turkey
- 1 egg
- ¼ teaspoon dried thyme
- ¼ teaspoon dried oregano
- ¼ teaspoon dried rosemary
- ¼ teaspoon garlic powder
- Salt and freshly ground black pepper, to taste
- 1½ cups tomato sauce

Method:

1. In a bowl, add all ingredients except tomato sauce and mix until well combined.
2. Make equal sized meatballs from the mixture.
3. In the bottom of Instant Pot, place meatballs and tomato sauce and gently stir to combine.
4. Secure the lid and place the pressure valve to "Seal" position.
5. Select "Manual" and cook under "High Pressure" for about 25 minutes.
6. Select the "Cancel" and carefully do a "Quick" release.
7. Remove the lid and serve.

Meal Prep Tip: Transfer the meatballs into a baking sheet and keep aside to cool completely. Divide the meatballs into 8 containers evenly. Cover the containers and refrigerate for up to 4 days. Reheat in the microwave before serving.

Nutritional Value per Serving:

- *Calories 101*
- *Total Fat 4.7 g*
- *Saturated Fat 1.5 g*
- *Cholesterol 61 mg*
- *Sodium 311 mg*
- *Total Carbs 2.7 g*
- *Fiber 0.8 g*
- *Sugar 2 g*
- *Protein 12.5 g*
- *Potassium 349 mg*

Chicken Meatballs

Preparation Time: 15 minutes

Cooking Time: 10 minutes

Servings: 8

Ingredients:

- 1-pound ground chicken
- 1 egg
- 1/3 cup almond flour
- ½ teaspoon garlic powder
- Salt and freshly ground black pepper, to taste
- ¾ cup hot sauce
- 2 tablespoons olive oil
- 2 tablespoons butter, melted
- ½ cup blue cheese dressing

Method:

1. In a bowl, add chicken, egg, almond flour, garlic powder, salt and black pepper and mix until well combined.
2. Make equal sized meatballs from the mixture.
3. Place the oil in the Instant Pot and select "Sauté". Then add the meatballs and cook for about 4-5 minutes or until browned from all sides.
4. Meanwhile, in a bowl, mix together hot sauce and butter.
5. Select the "Cancel" and place butter mixture over meatballs.
6. Secure the lid and place the pressure valve to "Seal" position.
7. Select the "Poultry" and just use the default time of 5 minutes.
8. Select the "Cancel" and carefully do a "Quick" release.
9. Remove the lid and serve immediately with the topping of dressing.

Meal Prep Tip: Transfer the meatballs into a baking sheet and keep aside to cool completely. Divide the meatballs into 8 containers evenly. Cover the containers and refrigerate for up to 4 days. Reheat in the microwave before serving. Top with blue cheese and serve.

Nutritional Value per Serving:

- *Calories 279*
- *Cholesterol 81 mg*
- *Fiber 0.6 g*
- *Sugar 0.8 g*
- *Protein 29 g*

Sweet & Sour Chicken Wings

Preparation Time: 15 minutes

Cooking Time: 15 minutes

Servings: 5

Ingredients:

- 1½ pounds chicken wings
- ¼ cup tomato puree
- 1 tablespoon honey
- 1 tablespoon fresh lemon juice
- Salt and freshly ground black pepper, to taste

Method:

1. In the bottom of Instant Pot, arrange a steamer trivet and pour 1 cup of water.
2. Place chicken wings on top of trivet, standing vertically.
3. Secure the lid and place the pressure valve to "Seal" position.
4. Select "Manual" and cook under "High Pressure" for about 10 minutes.
5. Preheat the oven to broiler.
6. Select the "Cancel" and carefully do a Quick release.
7. Meanwhile, in a bowl, add remaining ingredients and beat until well combined.
8. Remove the lid and transfer chicken wings into the bowl of sauce.
9. Coat the wings with sauce generously.
10. Arrange the chicken wings onto a parchment paper lined baking sheet and broil for about 5 minutes.
11. Serve hot with remaining sauce.

Meal Prep Tip: Transfer the wings into a bowl and keep aside to cool completely. Divide the wings into 5 containers evenly. Cover the containers and refrigerate for up to 3-4 days. Reheat in the microwave before serving.

Nutritional Value per Serving:

- *Calories 277*
- *Total Fat 10.1 g*
- *Saturated Fat 2.8 g*
- *Cholesterol 121 mg*
- *Sodium 152 mg*
- *Total Carbs 4.6 g*
- *Fiber 0.3 g*
- *Sugar 4.1 g*

BBQ Wings

Preparation Time: 15 minutes

Cooking Time: 20 minutes

Servings: 6

Ingredients:

- 2 pounds chicken wings and drumettes
- ½ cup BBQ sauce

Method:

1. In the bottom of Instant Pot, arrange a steamer basket and pour 1 cup of water.
2. Place the wings and drumettes into steamer basket.
3. Secure the lid and place the pressure valve to "Seal" position.
4. Select "Manual" and cook under "High Pressure" for about 5 minutes.
5. Preheat the oven to 450 degrees F. Arrange a wire rack in a baking sheet.
6. Select the "Cancel" and carefully do a Natural release.
7. Remove the lid and transfer wings and drumettes onto a large plate.
8. With paper towels, pat dry the wings and drumettes.
9. In a bowl, add wings and drumettes with BBQ sauce and toss to coat well.
10. Place the wings and drumettes onto prepared baking sheet in a single layer.
11. Bake for about 8-15 minutes.
12. Remove from oven and serve warm.

Meal Prep Tip: Transfer the wings into a bowl and keep aside to cool completely. Divide the wings into 5 containers evenly. Cover the containers and refrigerate for up to 3-4 days. Reheat in the microwave before serving.

Nutritional Value per Serving:

- *Calories 319*
- *Total Fat 11.3 g*
- *Saturated Fat 3.1 g*
- *Cholesterol 135 mg*
- *Sodium 363 mg*
- *Total Carbs 7.6 g*
- *Fiber 0.1 g*
- *Sugar 5.4 g*
- *Protein 43.7 g*
- *Potassium 411 mg*

Tomato Salsa

Preparation Time: 15 minutes

Cooking Time: 20 minutes

Servings: 20

Ingredients:

- 4 cups tomatoes, cored, peeled and chopped
- 1 (15-ounce) can tomato sauce
- 1 (6-ounce) can tomato paste
- 1 medium yellow onion, chopped
- 2 large green bell peppers, seeded and chopped
- 3 jalapeño peppers, seeded and chopped
- 4 garlic cloves, minced
- ½ cup apple cider vinegar
- 1 tablespoon hot sauce
- 1 tablespoon ground cumin
- Salt, to taste

Method:

1. In the pot of Instant Pot, place all ingredients and stir to combine.
2. Secure the lid and place the pressure valve to "Seal" position.
3. Select "Manual" and cook under "High Pressure" for about 15 minutes.
4. Select the "Cancel" and carefully do a "Natural" release.
5. Remove the lid and keep aside to cool for about 20 minutes.
6. Transfer the salsa into wide mouth pint jars and seal with lids.
7. Refrigerate to chill before serving.

Meal Prep Tip: Transfer the hot salsa into hot jars, leaving ½ inch of headspace. jars, leaving about ¼-½-inch space from the top. With a moist paper towel, wipe the rims of the jars to remove any food residue. Run a knife around the insides of the jars to remove any air bubbles. Top each jar with the lids and screw on rings. Process jars in a boiling water bath for about 15 minutes. Remove the jars from the pan and place onto a wood surface, several inches apart to cool completely. Place these jars in a cool, dark place to store. The opened jars can be preserved in refrigerator for up to 3 weeks.

Nutritional Value per Serving:

- *Calories 20*
- *Fiber 1.5 g*
- *Sugar 3.8 g*

Chickpeas Hummus

Preparation Time: 20 minutes
Cooking Time: 25 minutes
Servings: 14

Ingredients:

- 1 cup dried chickpeas, soaked for 12 hours and drained
- 4 cups water
- Salt, to taste
- ½ cup tahini
- 2 garlic cloves, chopped
- 3 tablespoons fresh lemon juice
- ¼ teaspoon ground cumin
- 2 tablespoons extra-virgin olive oil
- ¼ teaspoon paprika

Method:

1. In the pot of Instant Pot, place the chickpeas, water and 1 teaspoon of salt.
2. Secure the lid and place the pressure valve to "Seal" position.
3. Select "Bean/Chili" and just use the default time of 25 minutes.
4. Select the "Cancel" and carefully do a "Natural" release for about 15 minutes and then do a "Quick" release.
5. Remove the lid and drain the chickpeas, reserving about ¾ cup of the cooking liquid.
6. In a food processor, add the chickpeas, reserved cooking liquid, tahini, garlic, lemon juice, cumin, and salt and pulse at medium speed for until smooth and creamy.

Meal Prep Tip: Transfer hummus into airtight containers. Cover the containers and refrigerate for up to 6-7 days. Just before serving, drizzle with oil and sprinkle with paprika.
The opened jars can be preserved in refrigerator for up to 3 weeks.

Nutritional Value per Serving:

- *Calories 122*
- *Total Fat 7.5 g*
- *Saturated Fat 1.1 g*
- *Cholesterol 0 mg*
- *Sodium 28 mg*
- *Total Carbs 10.7 g*
- *Fiber 3.3 g*
- *Sugar 1.6 g*

CHAPTER 10: POULTRY RECIPES

Pulled Chicken

Preparation Time: 15 minutes

Cooking Time: 31 minutes

Servings: 8

Ingredients:

- 3 (6-ounce) boneless, skinless chicken breasts
- ½ cup water
- 1 tablespoon olive oil
- ½ onion, minced
- 3 garlic cloves, minced
- 1 (14-ounce) can coconut milk
- 2 teaspoons smoked paprika
- 1½ teaspoons ground cumin
- Salt and freshly ground black pepper, to taste

Method:

1. In the pot of Instant Pot, place chicken breasts and water.
2. Secure the lid and place the pressure valve to "Seal" position.
3. Select "Manual" and cook under "High Pressure" for about 26 minutes.
4. Select the "Cancel" and carefully do a "Quick" release.
5. Remove the lid and transfer the chicken breasts onto a cutting board.
6. With 2 forks, shred the chicken.
7. Drain the water from Instant Pot and with paper towels, pat dry it.
8. Place the coconut oil in the Instant Pot and select "Sauté". Then add the onion and garlic and cook for about 2-3 minutes.
9. Add the shredded chicken, coconut milk and spices and cook for about 1-2 minutes.
10. Select the "Cancel" and serve immediately.

Meal Prep Tip: Transfer the chicken mixture into a large bowl and keep aside to cool completely. Divide the chicken mixture into 8 containers evenly. Cover the containers and refrigerate for up to 3-4 days. Reheat in the microwave before serving.

Nutritional Value per Serving:

- *Calories 258*
- *Cholesterol 57 mg*
- *Total Carbs 4.2 g*

Glazed Chicken

Preparation Time: 15 minutes
Cooking Time: 22 minutes
Servings: 8
Ingredients:

- ½ cup soy sauce
- ¼ cup applesauce
- 2 tablespoons fish sauce
- 1 tablespoon white vinegar
- 1 teaspoon sesame oil
- 2 scallions, chopped
- 4 garlic cloves, minced
- 1 teaspoon fresh ginger, grated
- 3 pounds boneless, skinless chicken thighs

Method:

1. In a bowl, add all the ingredients except chicken and beat until well combined.
2. In the pot of Instant Pot, place the chicken and top with the honey mixture.
3. Secure the lid and place the pressure valve to "Seal" position.
4. Select "Manual" and cook under "High Pressure" for about 22 minutes.
5. Select the "Cancel" and carefully do a "Natural" release for about 10 minutes and then do a "Quick" release.
6. Remove the lid and stir the mixture well.
7. Serve hot.

Meal Prep Tip: Transfer the chicken mixture into a large bowl and keep aside to cool completely. Divide the mixture into 8 containers evenly. Cover the containers and refrigerate for up to 4 days. Reheat in the microwave before serving.

Nutritional Value per Serving:

- *Calories 219*
- *Total Fat 7.4 g*
- *Saturated Fat 1.6 g*
- *Cholesterol 143 mg*
- *Sodium 1390 mg*
- *Total Carbs 3.2 g*
- *Fiber 0.4 g*
- *Sugar 1.3 g*

Chicken with Pears

Preparation Time: 15 minutes

Cooking Time: 20 minutes

Servings: 8

Ingredients:

- 2 pounds boneless chicken breasts
- 2 tablespoons balsamic vinegar
- ½ tablespoon light brown sugar
- Salt and freshly ground black pepper, to taste
- 18¾-ounce canned sliced pears
- 1 cup fresh mushrooms, sliced

Method:

1. In the pot of Instant Pot, place all ingredients except pears and mushrooms.
2. Secure the lid and place the pressure valve to "Seal" position.
3. Select "Manual" and cook under "High Pressure" for about 10 minutes.
4. Select the "Cancel" and carefully do a "Natural" release.
5. Remove the lid and stir in the pears and mushrooms.
6. Secure the lid and place the pressure valve to "Seal" position.
7. Select "Manual" and cook under "High Pressure" for about 5 minutes.
8. Select the "Cancel" and carefully do a "Natural" release for about 5 minutes and then do a "Quick" release.
9. Remove the lid and select "Sauté".
10. Cook for about 5 minutes.
11. Select the "Cancel" and serve hot.

Meal Prep Tip: Transfer the chicken mixture into a large bowl and keep aside to cool completely. Divide the mixture into 8 containers evenly. Cover the containers and refrigerate for up to 4 days. Reheat in the microwave before serving.

Nutritional Value per Serving:

- *Calories 259*
- *Total Fat 8.5 g*
- *Saturated Fat 2.3 g*
- *Cholesterol 101 mg*
- *Sodium 119 mg*
- *Total Carbs 11 g*
- *Fiber 2.2 g*

Herbed Chicken

Preparation Time: 15 minutes
Cooking Time: 15 minutes
Servings: 6

Ingredients:

- 1 cup buttermilk
- 1 tablespoon honey
- 1 tablespoon Dijon mustard
- 1 teaspoon dried rosemary
- 1 teaspoon dried thyme
- 1 teaspoon dried sage
- Salt and freshly ground black pepper, to taste
- 2 pounds boneless, quarter chicken breasts

Method:

1. For marinade: in a large bowl, add all ingredients except chicken and mix until well combined.
2. Add chicken and coat with marinade generously.
3. Refrigerate for about 1-2 hours.
4. In the pot of Instant Pot, place chicken with marinade.
5. Secure the lid and place the pressure valve to "Seal" position.
6. Select "Manual" and cook under "High Pressure" for about 15 minutes.
7. Select the "Cancel" and carefully do a "Natural" release for about 5 minutes and then do a "Quick" release.
8. Remove the lid and serve hot.

Meal Prep Tip: Transfer the chicken mixture into a large bowl and keep aside to cool completely. Divide the mixture into 6 containers evenly. Cover the containers and refrigerate for up to 2-3 days. Reheat in the microwave before serving.

Nutritional Value per Serving:

- *Calories 191*
- *Total Fat 2.5 g*
- *Saturated Fat 0.3 g*
- *Cholesterol 89 mg*
- *Sodium 200 mg*
- *Total Carbs 5.3 g*
- *Fiber 0.3 g*

Chicken & Kale Soup

Preparation Time: 20 minutes

Cooking Time: 13 minutes

Servings: 5

Ingredients:

- 2 tablespoons olive oil
- 4 cups celery stalks, chopped
- 3 carrots, peeled and chopped
- 1 medium onion, chopped
- 2 bay leaves
- ¼ teaspoon dried oregano
- ¼ teaspoon dried thyme
- Salt and freshly ground black pepper, to taste
- 4 cups chicken broth
- 1 cup water
- 1 pound cooked chicken, shredded
- 2 cups fresh kale, trimmed and chopped
- ½ teaspoon Worcestershire sauce

Method:

1. Place the oil in the Instant Pot and select "Sauté". Then add the celery, carrot and onion and cook for about 5 minutes.
2. Add the bay leaves, herbs, salt and black pepper and cook for about 1 minute.
3. Select the "Cancel" and stir in the broth and water.
4. Secure the lid and place the pressure valve to "Seal" position.
5. Select "Soup" and just use the default time of 4 minutes.
6. Select the "Cancel" and carefully do a "Quick" release.
7. Remove the lid and select "Sauté".
8. Stir in the chicken and kale and cook for about 2-3 minutes.
9. Select the "Cancel" and stir in the Worcestershire sauce.
10. Serve hot.

Meal Prep Tip: Transfer the soup into a large bowl and keep aside to cool. Divide the mixture into 5 containers evenly. Cover the containers and refrigerate for 1-2 days. Reheat in the microwave before serving.

Nutritional Value per Serving:

- *Calories 267*

- Total Fat 9.6 g
- Saturated Fat 1.9 g
- Cholesterol 70 mg
- Sodium 808 mg
- Total Carbs 11.8 g
- Fiber 3.1 g
- Sugar 4.5 g
- Protein 32.1 g
- Potassium 828 mg

Chicken Chili

Preparation Time: 15 minutes

Cooking Time: 18 minutes

Servings: 5

Ingredients:

- 1 tablespoon olive oil
- 1 cup onion, chopped
- 1 teaspoon garlic, minced
- 1 teaspoon ground cumin, divided
- 1 pound boneless, skinless chicken thighs
- 1 cup bell pepper, seeded and chopped
- 1 (4-ounce) can green chiles
- 1¼ cups salsa Verde
- 2/3 cup corn
- 3 corn tortillas, chopped
- Salt and freshly ground black pepper, to taste
- 1½ cups chicken broth

Method:

1. Place the oil in the Instant Pot and select "Sauté". Then add the onion, garlic and ¼ teaspoon of cumin and cook for about 1-2 minutes.
2. Add chicken and cook for about 6 minutes.
3. Select the "Cancel" and stir in ½ teaspoon of cumin and remaining ingredients.
4. Secure the lid and place the pressure valve to "Seal" position.
5. Select "Manual" and cook under "High Pressure" for about 10 minutes.
6. Select the "Cancel" and carefully do a "Natural" release for about 10 minutes and then do a "Quick" release.
7. Remove the lid and stir the chili well.
8. Serve hot.

Meal Prep Tip: Transfer the chili into a large bowl and keep aside to cool. Divide the mixture into 5 containers evenly. Cover the containers and refrigerate for 1-2 days. Reheat in the microwave before serving.

Nutritional Value per Serving:

- *Calories 317*
- *Total Fat 11.1 g*
- *Saturated Fat 2.5 g*

- Cholesterol 81 mg
- Sodium 1190 mg
- Total Carbs 22.1 g
- Fiber 2.9 g
- Sugar 6 g
- Protein 31.5 g
- Potassium 453 mg

Turkey Bolognese Sauce

Preparation Time: 20 minutes

Cooking Time: 35 minutes

Servings: 6

Ingredients:

- 2 tablespoons olive oil
- 10-ounce fresh mushrooms, trimmed and chopped finely
- 2 celery stalks, chopped finely
- 2 carrots, peeled and chopped finely
- 1 medium onion, chopped finely
- 2 garlic cloves, chopped finely
- 1 pound 93% lean ground turkey
- ½ cup red wine
- 1 (28-ounce) can crushed tomatoes
- 1 bay leaf
- 1 teaspoon dried thyme
- Salt and freshly ground black pepper, to taste

Method:

1. Place the oil in the Instant Pot and select "Sauté". Then add the
2. Add chopped vegetables and cook for about 4-5 minutes.
3. Add ground turkey and cook for about 8-10 minutes, breaking up with a wooden spoon.
4. Add red wine and scrape the brown bits from the bottom.
5. Select the "Cancel" and stir in the remaining ingredients.
6. Secure the lid and place the pressure valve to "Seal" position.
7. Select "Manual" and cook under "High Pressure" for about 20 minutes.
8. Select the "Cancel" and carefully do a "Natural" release for about 10 minutes and then do a "Quick" release.
9. Remove the lid and serve hot with your favorite pasta.

Meal Prep Tip: Transfer the sauce into a large bowl and keep aside to cool completely. Divide the sauce into 4 containers evenly. Cover the containers and refrigerate for up to 1-2 days. You can also preserve cooked pasta in separate containers for about 1 day. Reheat the sauce in the microwave before serving.

Nutritional Value per Serving:

- *Calories 217*
- *Total Fat 10.5 g*

- *Saturated Fat 2.1 g*
- *Cholesterol 57 mg*
- *Sodium 107 mg*
- *Total Carbs 11.6 g*
- *Fiber 3.1 g*
- *Sugar 6.3 g*
- *Protein 17.3 g*
- *Potassium 595 mg*

CHAPTER 11: MEAT RECIPES

Beef with Broccoli

Preparation Time: 15 minutes

Cooking Time: 22 minutes

Servings: 6

Ingredients:

- 1½ pounds boneless beef chuck roast, cut into thin strips
- 1 onion, chopped
- 4 garlic cloves, minced
- ½ cup beef broth
- 1/3 cup low-sodium soy sauce
- 2 tablespoons honey
- 2 tablespoons sesame oil
- ¼ teaspoon red pepper flakes, crushed
- 12-ounce broccoli florets
- 2 tablespoons cornstarch
- 2 tablespoons water

Method:

1. In the pot of Instant Pot, place the beef, onion, garlic, broth, soy sauce, honey, sesame oil and red pepper flakes and stir to combine well.
2. Secure the lid and place the pressure valve to "Seal" position.
3. Select "Manual" and cook under "High Pressure" for about 12 minutes.
4. Select the "Cancel" and carefully do a "Quick" release.
5. Remove the lid and immediately, place the broccoli on top of beef mixture.
6. Immediately, secure the lid and place the pressure valve to "Seal" position for about 5 minutes.
7. Meanwhile, in a small bowl, dissolve the cornstarch in water.
8. Remove the lid and select "Sauté".
9. Stir in cornstarch mixture and cook for about 1-2 minutes.
10. Select the "Cancel" and serve hot.

Meal Prep Tip: Transfer the beef mixture into a large bowl and keep aside to cool completely. Divide the mixture into 6 containers evenly. Cover the containers and refrigerate for up to 3-4 days. Reheat in the microwave before serving.

Nutritional Value per Serving:

- *Calories 320*
- *Total Fat 11.9 g*
- *Saturated Fat 3.3 g*
- *Cholesterol 101 mg*
- *Sodium 941 mg*
- *Total Carbs 15.4 g*
- *Fiber 2 g*
- *Sugar 8.5 g*
- *Protein 37.7 g*
- *Potassium 694 mg*

Beef with Green Beans

Preparation Time: 15 minutes

Cooking Time: 30 minutes

Servings: 4

Ingredients:

For Spice Blend:

- 1 tablespoon ground cinnamon
- 1 teaspoon ground nutmeg
- ¼ teaspoon ground allspice
- Salt and freshly ground black pepper, to taste

For Beef Mixture:

- 1-pound beef chuck roast, cut in 2-inch chunks
- 1 pound fresh green beans, trimmed and cut in 2-inch pieces
- 1 medium onion, chopped
- 32-ounce canned tomato sauce

Method:

1. For spice blend: in a bowl, mix together all the ingredients.
2. In the pot of Instant Pot, place the spice blend and remaining all ingredients and stir to combine.
3. Secure the lid and place the pressure valve to "Seal" position.
4. Select "Meat/Stew" and just use the default time of 30 minutes.
5. Select the "Cancel" and carefully do a "Natural" release.
6. Remove the lid and serve hot.

Meal Prep Tip: Transfer the beef mixture into a large bowl and keep aside to cool completely. Divide the mixture into 4 containers evenly. Cover the containers and refrigerate for up to 3-4 days. Reheat in the microwave before serving.

Nutritional Value per Serving:

- *Calories 319*
- *Total Fat 7.9 g*
- *Saturated Fat 2.9 g*
- *Cholesterol 101 mg*
- *Sodium 1300 mg*
- *Total Carbs 24.6 g*
- *Fiber 8.9 g*
- *Sugar 12.6 g*

Beef with Bell Peppers

Preparation Time: 20 minutes

Cooking Time: 30 minutes

Servings: 5

Ingredients:

- 1-pound boneless beef, trimmed and cut into thin strips
- Salt and freshly ground black pepper, to taste
- 1 tablespoon olive oil
- 2 cups tomatoes, chopped
- 1½ cups tomato sauce
- 3 garlic cloves, minced
- 1 teaspoon dried rosemary
- 1 cup water
- 1 large green bell pepper, seeded and sliced into ½-inch thick strips
- 1 large red bell pepper, seeded and sliced into ½-inch thick strips
- 1 large yellow bell pepper, seeded and sliced into ½-inch thick strips

Method:

1. Season the beef with a little salt and black pepper.
2. Place the oil in the Instant Pot and select "Sauté". Then add the beef and cook for about 5 minutes.
3. Select the "Cancel" and transfer the beef into a bowl.
4. Now, add the tomatoes, tomato sauce, garlic, rosemary, salt, black pepper and water and stir to combine.
5. Place beef on top, followed by bell peppers.
6. Secure the lid and place the pressure valve to "Seal" position.
7. Select "Manual" and cook under "High Pressure" for about 25 minutes.
8. Select the "Cancel" and carefully do a "Quick" release.
9. Remove the lid and serve hot.

Meal Prep Tip: Transfer the beef mixture into a large bowl and keep aside to cool completely. Divide the beef mixture into 5 containers evenly. Cover the containers and refrigerate for up to 3-4 days. Reheat in the microwave before serving.

Nutritional Value per Serving:

- *Calories 249*
- *Total Fat 9 g*
- *Saturated Fat 2.6 g*

- Cholesterol 81 mg
- Sodium 483 mg
- Total Carbs 12.9 g
- Fiber 3.1 g
- Sugar 8.6 g
- Protein 30 g
- Potassium 924 mg

Beef in Pear Sauce

Preparation Time: 15 minutes

Cooking Time: 45 minutes

Servings: 7

Ingredients:

- 1 (14-ounce) can pears, drained
- 4 garlic cloves, peeled
- 1 teaspoon fresh ginger, chopped roughly
- ¼ cup brown sugar
- ½ cup soy sauce
- 1 teaspoon sesame oil
- 2 pounds top sirloin, trimmed and cut into large chunks

Method:

1. In a food processor, add the pears, garlic, ginger, brown sugar, soy sauce and sesame oil and pulse until smooth.
2. In the pot of Instant Pot, place the beef and top with half of the pureed mixture.
3. Secure the lid and place the pressure valve to "Seal" position.
4. Select "Manual" and cook under "High Pressure" for about 45 minutes.
5. Select the "Cancel" and carefully do a "Natural" release.
6. Remove the lid and with 2 forks, shred the meat.
7. Serve the shredded beef in tortillas with your desired topping alongside the remaining pureed mixture.

Meal Prep Tip: Transfer the beef mixture into a large bowl and keep aside to cool completely. Divide the beef mixture into 7 containers evenly. Cover the containers and refrigerate for up to 3-4 days. Reheat in the microwave before serving.

Nutritional Value per Serving:

- *Calories 312*
- *Total Fat 8.9 g*
- *Saturated Fat 3.2 g*
- *Cholesterol 116 mg*
- *Sodium 1114 mg*
- *Total Carbs 15.9 g*
- *Fiber 2 g*
- *Sugar 10.9 g*
- *Protein 40.8 g*

Beef in Spicy Sauce

Preparation Time: 15 minutes

Cooking Time: 35 minutes

Servings: 6

Ingredients:

For Beef:

- 1 teaspoon red chili powder
- 1 teaspoon red pepper flakes
- 1 teaspoon ground cumin
- 1 teaspoon ground coriander
- Salt and freshly ground black pepper, to taste
- 2 pounds beef chuck roast, cut into 1½-inch cubes

For Sauce:

- 1½ cups beef broth
- 1 medium onion, chopped
- 2 garlic cloves, chopped
- 2 tablespoons fresh lemon juice
- Salt and freshly ground black pepper, to taste

Method:

1. For spice mixture: in a small bowl, mix together all ingredients except roast.
2. Rub chuck roast with spice mixture generously.
3. For sauce: in a food processor, add all ingredients and pulse until smooth.
4. In the pot of Instant Pot, place the roast and top with sauce evenly.
5. Secure the lid and place the pressure valve to "Seal" position.
6. Select "Meat/Stew" and just use the default time of 35 minutes.
7. Select the "Cancel" and carefully do a "Natural" release.
8. Remove the lid and serve with the topping of pan sauce.

Meal Prep Tip: Transfer the beef mixture into a large bowl and keep aside to cool completely. Divide the beef mixture into 16 containers evenly. Cover the containers and refrigerate for up to 3-4 days. Reheat in the microwave before serving.

Nutritional Value per Serving:

- *Calories 304*
- *Total Fat 10 g*
- *Saturated Fat 3.7 g*
- *Cholesterol 135 mg*

- Sodium 324 mg
- Total Carbs 2.9 g
- Fiber 0.7 g
- Sugar 1.1 g
- Protein 47.5 g
- Potassium 719 mg

Tangy Flank Steak

Preparation Time: 15 minutes

Cooking Time: 41 minutes

Servings: 6

Ingredients:

- ¼ cup olive oil, divided
- 2 pounds flank steak
- ¼ cup apple cider vinegar
- 1 tablespoon Worcestershire sauce
- 2 tablespoons dried onion soup mix

Method:

1. Place 1 tablespoon of the oil in the Instant Pot and select "Sauté". Then add the flank steak and cook for about 2-3 minutes per side.
2. Select the "Cancel" and stir in the remaining oil, vinegar, Worcestershire sauce and onion soup mix.
3. Secure the lid and place the pressure valve to "Seal" position.
4. Select "Manual" and cook under "High Pressure" for about 35 minutes.
5. Select the "Cancel" and carefully do a "Natural" release for about 5 minutes and then do a "Quick" release.
6. Remove the lid and transfer the steak onto a cutting board.
7. Cut into desired sized slices and stir with the pot sauce.
8. Serve hot.

Meal Prep Tip: Transfer the steak mixture into a large bowl and keep aside to cool completely. Divide the mixture into 4 containers evenly. Cover the containers and refrigerate for up to 3-4 days. Reheat in the microwave before serving.

Nutritional Value per Serving:

- *Calories 268*
- *Total Fat 15.1 g*
- *Saturated Fat 3.9 g*
- *Cholesterol 744 mg*
- *Sodium 233 mg*
- *Total Carbs 1.3 g*
- *Fiber 0 g*
- *Sugar 0.9 g*

Pulled Beef with Pepperoncini

Preparation Time: 15 minutes

Cooking Time: 1 hour 10 minutes

Servings: 16

Ingredients:

- 1 tablespoon olive oil
- 5 pounds chuck roast
- 1 (16-ounce) jar sliced pepperoncini peppers
- ½ yellow onion, sliced thinly
- 1 package Italian dressing seasoning mix
- 1 cup water

Method:

1. Place the oil in the Instant Pot and select "Sauté". Then add the chuck roast and cook for about 5 minutes per side.
2. Select the "Cancel" and stir in half of the pepperoncini pepper jar, ¼ cup pepperoncini brine, onion, Italian seasoning mix and water.
3. Select the "Cancel" and stir in the remaining ingredients.
4. Secure the lid and place the pressure valve to "Seal" position.
5. Select "Manual" and cook under "High Pressure" for about 55-60 minutes.
6. Select the "Cancel" and carefully do a "Quick" release.
7. Remove the lid and with 2 forks, shred the meat.
8. Add the remaining pepperoncini peppers and stir to combine.
9. Serve according to your choice.

Meal Prep Tip: Transfer the beef mixture into a large bowl and keep aside to cool completely. Divide the beef mixture into 16 containers evenly. Cover the containers and refrigerate for up to 3-4 days. Reheat in the microwave before serving.

Nutritional Value per Serving:

- *Calories 288*
- *Total Fat 9.8 g*
- *Saturated Fat 3.5 g*
- *Cholesterol 127 mg*
- *Sodium 418 mg*
- *Total Carbs 4.4 g*
- *Fiber 0.1 g*
- *Sugar 1.2 g*

Spicy Pulled Beef

Preparation Time: 15 minutes

Cooking Time: 1 hour 10 minutes

Servings: 10

Ingredients:

- ½ medium onion
- 5 garlic cloves
- 3 tablespoons chipotles in adobo sauce
- 2 tablespoons fresh lime juice
- 1 tablespoon dried oregano, crushed
- 1 tablespoon ground cumin
- ½ teaspoon cayenne pepper
- ½ teaspoon ground cloves
- 1 cup water
- 3 pounds beef bottom round roast, trimmed and cut into 3-inch pieces
- Salt and freshly ground black pepper, to taste
- 1 teaspoon olive oil
- 3 bay leaves

Method:

1. In a blender, add onion, garlic, chipotles, lime juice, oregano, cumin, cloves, cayenne and water and pulse until smooth.
2. Season the beef with the salt and black pepper evenly.
3. Place the oil in the Instant Pot and select "Sauté". Then add the beef in batches and cook for about 5 minutes or until browned completely.
4. Select the "Cancel" and stir in the pureed mixture and bay leaves.
5. Secure the lid and place the pressure valve to "Seal" position.
6. Select "Manual" and cook under "High Pressure" for about 65 minutes.
7. Select the "Cancel" and carefully do a "Quick" release.
8. Remove the lid and transfer the meat a dish, reserving the cooking liquid.
9. With two forks, shred the met and transfer into a bowl.
10. Add 1½ cups of the reserved liquid and stir to combine.
11. Serve according to your choice.

Meal Prep Tip: Transfer the beef mixture into a large bowl and keep aside to cool completely. Divide the beef mixture into 10 containers evenly. Cover the containers and refrigerate for up to 3-4 days. Reheat in the microwave before serving.

Nutritional Value per Serving:

- Calories 266
- Total Fat 9.2 g
- Saturated Fat 3.3 g
- Cholesterol 122 mg
- Sodium 108 mg
- Total Carbs 1.8 g
- Fiber 0.5 g
- Sugar 0.3 g
- Protein 41.6 g
- Potassium 586 mg

Fruity Pulled Beef

Preparation Time: 15 minutes

Cooking Time: 1 hour 10 minutes

Servings: 12

Ingredients:

- 2 tablespoons olive oil
- 4 pounds bottom roast, cubed
- 1 cup low-sodium beef broth
- ½ cup low-sodium soy sauce
- 1 tablespoon fresh ginger, grated finely
- 5 garlic cloves, minced
- 1 Granny Smith apple, peeled, cored and chopped finely
- Freshly ground black pepper, to taste
- ¼ cup fresh orange juice

Method:

1. Place the oil in the Instant Pot and select "Sauté". Then add the beef cubes in 2 batches and cook for about 4-5 minutes.
2. Select the "Cancel" and stir in the remaining ingredients.
3. Secure the lid and place the pressure valve to "Seal" position.
4. Select "Manual" and cook under "Normal Pressure" for about 45 minutes.
5. Select the "Cancel" and carefully do a "Quick" release.
6. Remove the lid and with 2 forks, shred the beef.
7. Serve hot with the pan sauce.

Meal Prep Tip: Transfer the beef mixture into a large bowl and keep aside to cool completely. Divide the beef mixture into 12 containers evenly. Cover the containers and refrigerate for up to 3-4 days. Reheat in the microwave before serving.

Nutritional Value per Serving:

- *Calories 320*
- *Total Fat 11.8 g*
- *Saturated Fat 3.9 g*
- *Cholesterol 135 mg*
- *Sodium 724 mg*
- *Total Carbs 4.5 g*
- *Sugar 3.1 g*
- *Protein 47g*

Meatballs with Mushroom Sauce

Preparation Time: 15 minutes

Cooking Time: 22 minutes

Servings: 6

Ingredients:

- 1-pound ground beef
- ½ pound ground pork
- 2 tablespoons dried onion, minced
- ¼ cup fresh parsley, minced
- 2 teaspoons dried sage
- ½ teaspoon fennel seeds, crushed
- ½ teaspoon ground nutmeg
- ½ teaspoon garlic powder
- Salt and freshly ground black pepper, to taste
- 8-ounce fresh button mushrooms, sliced
- 1 large onion, chopped
- ¼ cup beef broth
- ¼ cup low-sodium soy sauce
- 2 tablespoons arrowroot powder
- ½ cup full-fat coconut milk

Method:

1. In a large bowl, add the beef, pork, dried onion, parsley, sage, fennel seeds, nutmeg, garlic powder, salt and black pepper and mix until well combined.
2. Make 1-inch meatballs from the mixture.
3. In the pot of Instant Pot, place the mushrooms, onion, broth and soy sauce and stir to combine.
4. Arrange the meatballs on top of the mushroom mixture.
5. Secure the lid and place the pressure valve to "Seal" position.
6. Select "Meat/Stew" and just use the default time of 20 minutes.
7. Select the "Cancel" and carefully do a "Quick" release.
8. Meanwhile, in a small bowl, dissolve the arrowroot powder in coconut milk.
9. Remove the lid and select "Sauté".
10. Add the arrowroot powder mixture and gently, stir to combine.
11. Cook for about 1-2 minutes.
12. Select the "Cancel" and serve hot.

Meal Prep Tip: Transfer the meatballs mixture into a bowl and keep aside to cool completely. Divide the meatballs mixture into 6 containers evenly. Cover the containers and refrigerate for up to 4 days. Reheat in the microwave before serving.

Nutritional Value per Serving:
- Calories 280
- Total Fat 11.2 g
- Saturated Fat 6.2 g
- Cholesterol 98 mg
- Sodium 740 mg
- Total Carbs 6.8 g
- Fiber 1.2 g
- Sugar 2.3 g
- Protein 37.5 g
- Potassium 513 mg

Pork with Pineapple

Preparation Time: 15 minutes

Cooking Time: 18 minutes

Servings: 7

Ingredients:

- 1 (20-ounce) can pineapple chunks in juice
- 3 garlic cloves, minced
- 1 tablespoon fresh ginger, grated
- 3 tablespoons honey
- 2 tablespoons brown sugar
- 2 tablespoons soy sauce
- 2 tablespoons water
- 1 tablespoon cornstarch
- 2 tablespoons olive oil, divided
- 1 red bell pepper, seeded and chopped
- 1 onion, chopped
- 2 pounds boneless pork stew meat
- 1 teaspoon dried oregano
- Salt and freshly ground black pepper, to taste

Method:

1. Drain the pineapple chunks, reserving the juice in a bowl.
2. For the sauce: in the bowl of pineapple juice, add garlic, ginger, honey, brown sugar, soy sauce, water and cornstarch and beat until well combined.
3. Place 1 tablespoon of oil in the Instant Pot and select "Sauté". Then add the bell pepper and onion and cook for about 3 minutes.
4. Transfer the onion mixture into a bowl.
5. Place the remaining oil in the Instant Pot and select "Sauté". Then add the pork meat and cook for about 4-5 minutes.
6. Add pineapple chunks, oregano, salt and black pepper and stir to combine.
7. Select the "Cancel" and stir in the sauce.
8. Secure the lid and place the pressure valve to "Seal" position.
9. Select "Manual" and cook under "High Pressure" for about 10 minutes.
10. Select the "Cancel" and carefully do a "Natural" release for about 5 minutes and then do a "Quick" release.
11. Remove the lid and stir in the cooked onion mixture.
12. Serve hot.

Meal Prep Tip: Transfer the pork mixture into a large bowl and keep aside to cool completely. Divide the pork mixture into 7 containers evenly. Cover the containers and refrigerate for up to 1-2 days. Reheat in the microwave before serving.

Nutritional Value per Serving:

- Calories 321
- Total Fat 8.8 g
- Saturated Fat 2.2 g
- Cholesterol 95 mg
- Sodium 359 mg
- Total Carbs 25.8 g
- Fiber 2 g
- Sugar 19.5 g
- Protein 35.2 g
- Potassium 726 mg

Lamb in Yogurt Sauce

Preparation Time: 15 minutes

Cooking Time: 20 minutes

Servings: 4

Ingredients:

- 1 tablespoon olive oil
- 1 medium onion, chopped
- 1 tablespoon fresh ginger, crushed
- 1 tablespoon garlic, crushed
- 2 tablespoons tomato paste
- ¾ cup water, divided
- 1-pound lamb leg steak, cut into 1-inch pieces
- ½ cup plain yogurt
- 1 teaspoon ground cumin
- ½ teaspoon ground turmeric
- ½ teaspoon cayenne pepper
- ½ teaspoon paprika
- Salt and freshly ground black pepper, to taste
- 1 tablespoon fresh lime juice
- 2 tablespoons fresh cilantro, chopped

Method:

1. Place the ghee in the Instant Pot and select "Sauté". Then add the onion, ginger and garlic and cook for about 2-3 minutes.
2. Add tomato paste an ¼ cup of water and cook for about 1-2 minute.
3. Select the "Cancel" and stir in remaining water, lamb pieces, yogurt and spices.
4. Secure the lid and place the pressure valve to "Seal" position.
5. Select "Manual" and cook under "High Pressure" for about 15 minutes.
6. Select the "Cancel" and carefully do a "Natural" release.
7. Remove the lid and stir in lime juice.
8. Serve hot with the topping of cilantro.

Meal Prep Tip: Transfer the lamb mixture into a large bowl and keep aside to cool completely. Divide the lamb mixture into 4 containers evenly. Cover the containers and refrigerate for up to 1-2 days. Reheat in the microwave before serving.

Nutritional Value per Serving:

- *Calories 292*

- Total Fat 12.5 g
- Saturated Fat 3.8 g
- Cholesterol 104 mg
- Sodium 161 mg
- Total Carbs 8.7 g
- Fiber 1.5 g
- Sugar 4.4 g
- Protein 34.7 g
- Potassium 627 mg

Lamb Curry

Preparation Time: 15 minutes

Cooking Time: 12 minutes

Servings: 4

Ingredients:

- 1 tablespoon butter
- 1 teaspoon cumin seeds
- 1 large yellow onion, chopped
- 1 teaspoon grated garlic
- 1 teaspoon grated fresh ginger
- 1 tablespoon ground coriander
- 1 teaspoon red chili powder
- ½ tsp. ground turmeric
- 1-pound lean ground lamb
- 2 plum tomatoes, chopped finely
- ½ cup water
- ¼ cup fresh cilantro, chopped

Method:

1. Place the butter in the Instant Pot and select "Sauté". Then add the cumin seeds and sauté for about 30 seconds.
2. Add onion and cook for about 2-3 minutes.
3. Add garlic, ginger and spices and cook for about 1 minute.
4. Add lamb and cook for about 2-3 minutes.
5. Select the "Cancel" and stir in the tomatoes and water.
6. Secure the lid and place the pressure valve to "Seal" position.
7. Select "Manual" and cook under "High Pressure" for about 4 minutes.
8. Select the "Cancel" and carefully do a "Natural" release.
9. Remove the lid and serve hot with the garnishing of cilantro.

Meal Prep Tip: Transfer the lamb mixture into a large bowl and keep aside to cool completely. Divide the lamb mixture into 4 containers evenly. Cover the containers and refrigerate for up to 1-2 days. Reheat in the microwave before serving.

Nutritional Value per Serving:

- *Calories 273*
- *Total Fat 11.6 g*
- *Saturated Fat 4.9 g*

- Cholesterol 110 mg
- Sodium 125 mg
- Total Carbs 8 g
- Fiber 1.9 g
- Sugar 4.2 g
- Protein 33.3 g
- Potassium 600 mg

CHAPTER 12: VEGETARIAN RECIPES

Green Beans with Carrots

Preparation Time: 15 minutes

Cooking Time: 2 minutes

Servings: 2

Ingredients:

- 3-ounce fresh green beans, trimmed
- 4 small carrots, peeled and sliced into long sticks
- 1 large garlic clove, sliced
- Salt and freshly ground black pepper, to taste
- 1 tablespoon butter, melted
- 1 tablespoon lemon juice
- 1 lemon slice
- 1 tablespoon fresh rosemary, chopped

Method:

1. Arrange a parchment paper onto a smooth surface.
2. Place the green beans, carrots and garlic in the center of paper and sprinkle with the salt and pepper.
3. Drizzle with butter and lemon juice and top with the lemon slice and rosemary.
4. Fold the paper tightly to form a parcel.
5. Arrange a steamer trivet in the bottom of Instant Pot and pour 1 cup of water.
6. Place veggie parcel on top of trivet.
7. Secure the lid and place the pressure valve to "Seal" position.
8. Select "Manual" and cook under "High Pressure" for about 2 minutes.
9. Select the "Cancel" and carefully do a "Natural" release for about 3 minutes and then do a "Quick" release.
10. Remove the lid and serve hot.

Meal Prep Tip: Transfer the vegetable mixture into a large bowl and keep aside to cool completely. Divide the mixture into 2 containers evenly. Cover the containers and refrigerate for up to 2 days. Reheat in the microwave before serving.

Nutritional Value per Serving:

- *Calories 113*
- *Fiber 4.7 g*
- *Protein 1.8 g*

Mixed Veggie Combo

Preparation Time: 20 minutes

Cooking Time: 13 minutes

Servings: 6

Ingredients:

- 1 large eggplant, cubed
- Salt, to taste
- 3 tablespoons olive oil
- 2 medium potatoes, cubed
- 1 medium red bell pepper, seeded and cut into strips
- 1 onion, cut into thin wedges
- 2 medium zucchinis, cut into rounds
- ¼ cup olives, pitted
- 2 tablespoons fresh basil, chopped
- 1 tablespoon capers, strained and rinsed
- 2 tablespoons pine nuts, divided
- 1 tablespoon raisins, soaked in hot water and squeezed
- Freshly ground black pepper, to taste
- 1 cup water
- 10 cherry tomatoes, halved

Method:

1. In a strainer, place the eggplant and sprinkle with salt.
2. Place a heavy plate on top of the eggplant for about 30 minutes.
3. Place the oil in the Instant Pot and select "Sauté". Then add the eggplant and potatoes and cook for about 3 minutes.
4. Add bell pepper and onion and cook for about 3 minutes.
5. Add zucchinis and cook for about 3 minutes.
6. Select the "Cancel" and stir in the remaining ingredients except the cherry tomatoes.
7. Secure the lid and place the pressure valve to "Seal" position.
8. Select "Manual" and cook under "High Pressure" for about 4 minutes.
9. Select the "Cancel" and carefully do a "Natural" release.
10. Remove the lid and transfer the mixture into a serving dish.
11. Stir in cherry tomatoes and serve.

Meal Prep Tip: Transfer the cooked vegetable mixture into a large bowl and keep aside to cool completely. Divide the mixture into 6 containers evenly. Preserve cherry tomatoes in separate containers. Cover the containers and refrigerate for up to 2-3 days. Reheat in the microwave before serving.

Nutritional Value per Serving:

- Calories 2200
- Total Fat 10.4 g
- Saturated Fat 1.3 g
- Cholesterol 0 mg
- Sodium 143 mg
- Total Carbs 31 g
- Fiber 8. g
- Sugar 12.4 g
- Protein 5.5 g
- Potassium 1218 mg

Wine Braised Veggies

Preparation Time: 20 minutes

Cooking Time: 23 minutes

Servings: 8

Ingredients:

- 3 cups vegetable broth, divided
- 1¼ pounds Yukon gold potatoes, cut into bite-sized pieces
- 1-pound baby Bella mushrooms
- 2 cups frozen pearl onions
- 2 large carrots, peeled and cut into bite-sized pieces
- 4 garlic cloves, minced
- 3 fresh thyme sprigs
- ½ cup dry red wine
- 3 tablespoons tomato paste
- 2 tablespoons Worcestershire sauce
- Salt and freshly ground black pepper, to taste
- 2 tablespoons cornstarch

Method:

1. In the pot of Instant Pot, place 2½ cups of broth and remaining ingredients except the cornstarch and stir to combine.
2. Secure the lid and place the pressure valve to "Seal" position.
3. Select "Manual" and cook under "High Pressure" for about 20 minutes.
4. Select the "Cancel" and carefully do a "Natural" release for about 15 minutes and then do a "Quick" release.
5. Meanwhile, in a small bowl, dissolve the cornstarch into remaining broth.
6. Remove the lid and select "Sauté".
7. Stir in cornstarch mixture and cook for about 2-3 minutes.
8. Select the "Cancel" and serve hot.

Meal Prep Tip: Transfer the vegetable mixture into a large bowl and keep aside to cool completely. Divide the mixture into 8 containers evenly. Cover the containers and refrigerate for up to 2-3 days. Reheat in the microwave before serving.

Nutritional Value per Serving:

- *Calories 99*
- *Total Fat 0.7 g*
- *Saturated Fat 0.2 g*

- Cholesterol 0 mg
- Sodium 376 mg
- Total Carbs 16.6 g
- Fiber 2.2 g
- Sugar 5.1 g
- Protein 4.3 g
- Potassium 680 mg

Veggies Soup

Preparation Time: 15 minutes
Cooking Time: 15 minutes
Servings: 6

Ingredients:

- 3 cups green cabbage, chopped
- 1 (14½-ounce) can diced tomatoes
- 3 carrots, peeled and chopped
- 3 celery stalks, chopped
- 1 onion, chopped
- 2 garlic cloves, chopped
- 2 tablespoons apple cider vinegar
- 1 tablespoon fresh lemon juice
- 2 teaspoons dried sage
- Salt and freshly ground black pepper, to taste
- 2½ cups vegetable broth

Method:

1. In the pot of Instant Pot, place all the ingredients and stir to combine.
2. Secure the lid and place the pressure valve to "Seal" position.
3. Select "Manual" and cook under "High Pressure" for about 15 minutes.
4. Select the "Cancel" and carefully do a "Natural" release.
5. Remove the lid and serve hot.

Meal Prep Tip: Transfer the soup into a large bowl and keep aside to cool. Divide the mixture into 6 containers evenly. Cover the containers and refrigerate for 1-2 days. Reheat in the microwave before serving.

Nutritional Value per Serving:

- *Calories 113*
- *Total Fat 2.7 g*
- *Saturated Fat 0.7 g*
- *Sodium 1300 mg*
- *Total Carbs 11.8 g*
- *Fiber 3.1 g*
- *Sugar 6.6 g*

Veggies Curry

Preparation Time: 15 minutes

Cooking Time: 9 minutes

Servings: 4

Ingredients:

- 2 tomatoes, chopped roughly
- ½ small onion, chopped roughly
- 1 teaspoon fresh ginger, chopped roughly
- 7 garlic cloves, chopped roughly
- 1 serrano pepper
- 1 teaspoon olive oil
- 1 teaspoon ground cumin
- ½ teaspoon ground turmeric
- ½ teaspoon red chili powder
- 2 medium potatoes, cubed into small size
- 1 small cauliflower head, cut into large florets
- ¼ cup water

Method:

1. In a blender, add tomato, onion, ginger, garlic and serrano and pulse until smooth.
2. Place the oil in the Instant Pot and select "Sauté". Then add the tomato puree and cook for about 2-3 minutes.
3. Add the spices and potato and cook for about 3-4 minutes.
4. Select the "Cancel" and stir in cauliflower and water.
5. Secure the lid and place the pressure valve to "Seal" position.
6. Select "Manual" and cook under "Low Pressure" for about 2 minutes.
7. Select the "Cancel" and carefully do a "Quick" release.
8. Remove the lid and stir in lemon juice.
9. Serve hot.

Meal Prep Tip: Transfer the curry into a large bowl and keep aside to cool. Divide the mixture into 4 containers evenly. Cover the containers and refrigerate for 2-3 days. Reheat in the microwave before serving.

Nutritional Value per Serving:

- *Calories 129*
- *Total Fat 1.8 g*
- *Saturated Fat 0.3 g*

- *Cholesterol 0 mg*
- *Sodium 36 mg*
- *Total Carbs 26.2 g*
- *Fiber 5.6 g*
- *Sugar 5 g*
- *Protein 4.3 g*
- *Potassium 848 mg*

Quinoa Salad

Preparation Time: 15 minutes

Cooking Time: 1 minute

Servings: 5

Ingredients:

- 1 cup quinoa, rinsed
- 2 cups water
- ¼ cup olive oil
- ¼ cup fresh lemon juice
- Salt and freshly ground black pepper, to taste
- 1 red bell pepper, seeded and chopped finely
- ½ small red onion, chopped finely
- 2 cups tomatoes, chopped
- 1 cucumber, peeled, seeded and chopped
- 1 garlic clove, minced
- 1 bunch mint, chopped finely
- 1 bunch parsley, chopped finely

Method:

1. In the pot of Instant Pot, place the quinoa and water.
2. Secure the lid and place the pressure valve to "Seal" position.
3. Select "Manual" and cook under "High Pressure" for about 1 minute.
4. Select the "Cancel" and carefully do a "Natural" release for about 10 minutes and then do a "Quick" release.
5. Remove the lid and with a fork fluff the quinoa.
6. Transfer the quinoa into a large bowl with oil, lemon juice, salt, and pepper.
7. Keep aside to cool.
8. Add remaining ingredients except the herbs and mix well.
9. Refrigerate, covered for at least 1 hour.
10. Stir in the herbs and serve.

Meal Prep Tip: Divide the cooled quinoa mixture into 4 containers evenly. Reserve the raw vegetables in separate containers. Cover the containers and refrigerate for up to 1 week. Reheat in the microwave before serving.

Nutritional Value per Serving:

- *Calories1249*
- *Total Fat 12.6 g*

- *Saturated Fat 1.8 g*
- *Cholesterol 0 mg*
- *Sodium 45 mg*
- *Total Carbs 30 g*
- *Fiber 4.1 g*
- *Sugar 4.7 g*
- *Protein 6.4 g*
- *Potassium 543 mg*

Quinoa with Tofu

Preparation Time: 15 minutes

Cooking Time: 7 minutes

Servings: 8

Ingredients:

- 1 tablespoon olive oil
- 1 large onion, chopped
- 1 cup uncooked quinoa, rinsed
- 2 garlic cloves, minced
- ½ teaspoon fresh ginger, grated
- 1 teaspoon ground turmeric
- 1 teaspoon ground cumin
- 1 teaspoon ground coriander
- 2 cups low-sodium vegetable broth
- 12-ounce firm tofu, cut into ½-inch cubes
- 2 bell peppers, seeded and chopped
- 4 cups cauliflower rice
- ¼ cup fresh cilantro leaves
- ¼ cup almonds, toasted sliced
- 3 tablespoons fresh lemon juice
- Salt and freshly ground black pepper, to taste

Method:

1. Place the oil in the Instant Pot and select "Sauté". Then add the onion and cook for about 2-3 minutes.
2. Add the quinoa, garlic and ginger and stir for about 1-2 minutes.
3. Stir in the spices, salt and pepper and cook for about 30 seconds.
4. Stir in 2 tablespoons of broth and scrape the brown bits from the bottom.
5. Select the "Cancel" and stir in the tofu, bell pepper and remaining broth.
6. Secure the lid and place the pressure valve to "Seal" position.
7. Select "Manual" and cook under "High Pressure" for about 1 minutes.
8. Select the "Cancel" and carefully do a "Natural" release for about 5 minutes and then do a "Quick" release.
9. Remove the lid and stir in the cauliflower rice.
10. Secure the lid for about 5 minutes.
11. Remove the lid and stir in the almond, cilantro, lemon juice and serve warm.

Meal Prep Tip: Divide the cooled quinoa mixture into 8 containers evenly. Cover the containers and refrigerate for up to 1 week. Reheat in the microwave before serving.

Nutritional Value per Serving:
- Calories 178
- Total Fat 6.6 g
- Saturated Fat 1 g
- Cholesterol 0 mg
- Sodium 62 mg
- Total Carbs 22.7 g
- Fiber 4.4 g
- Sugar 4 g
- Protein 9.3 g
- Potassium 463 mg

Lentil Bolognese Sauce

Preparation Time: 15 minutes

Cooking Time: 5 minutes

Servings: 5

Ingredients:

- 1 (25-ounce) jar marinara sauce
- ¾ cup red lentils
- ½ cup water
- Salt and freshly ground black pepper, to taste

Method:

1. In the pot of Instant Pot, place marinara sauce, lentils and water and stir to combine.
2. Secure the lid and place the pressure valve to "Seal" position.
3. Select "Manual" and cook under "High Pressure" for about 5 minutes.
4. Select the "Cancel" and carefully do a "Natural" release for about 10 minutes and then do a "Quick" release.
5. Remove the lid and stir in the salt and pepper.
6. Serve warm over your favorite pasta or spiralized veggie noodles.

Meal Prep Tip: Transfer the lentil mixture into a large bowl and keep aside to cool completely. Divide the mixture into 4 containers evenly. Cover the containers and refrigerate for up to 5 days. Reheat in the microwave before serving.

Nutritional Value per Serving:

- *Calories 225*
- *Total Fat 4.1 g*
- *Saturated Fat 1 g*
- *Cholesterol 3 mg*
- *Sodium 615 mg*
- *Total Carbs 36.8 g*
- *Fiber 12.5 g*
- *Sugar 13.1 g*
- *Protein 10 g*
- *Potassium 723 mg*

Lentil Chili

Preparation Time: 15 minutes

Cooking Time: 19 minutes

Servings: 7

Ingredients:

- 1 tablespoon olive oil
- 2 carrots, peeled and chopped
- 1 onion, chopped
- 4 garlic cloves, minced
- 2 jalapeño peppers, chopped
- 1½ tablespoons red chili powder
- 1 tablespoon ground cumin
- ½ teaspoon ground coriander
- 1 teaspoon dried oregano
- Salt, to taste
- 1 (28-ounce) can fire roasted diced tomatoes
- 1 (15-ounce) can crushed tomatoes
- 2 cups green lentils
- 4 cups vegetable broth
- 1 teaspoon fresh lime juice

Method:

1. Place the oil in the Instant Pot and select "Sauté". Then add the carrots, onion, garlic and jalapeño peppers and cook for about 3-4 minutes.
2. Select the "Cancel" and stir in the remaining ingredients.
3. Secure the lid and place the pressure valve to "Seal" position.
4. Select "Manual" and cook under "High Pressure" for about 15 minutes.
5. Select the "Cancel" and carefully do a "Quick" release.
6. Remove the lid and stir in lime juice.
7. Serve hot.

Meal Prep Tip: Transfer the chili into a large bowl and keep aside to cool. Divide the mixture into 10 containers evenly. Cover the containers and refrigerate for 6-7 days. Reheat in the microwave before serving.

Nutritional Value per Serving:

- *Calories 318*

- Total Fat 4.9 g
- Saturated Fat 0.8 g
- Cholesterol 0 mg
- Sodium 764 mg
- Total Carbs 50.6 g
- Fiber 23.2 g
- Sugar 10 g
- Protein 20.8 g
- Potassium 1140 mg

Asparagus Risotto

Preparation Time: 15 minutes

Cooking Time: 12 minutes

Servings: 8

Ingredients:

- 2 tablespoons unsalted butter
- 2 cups onion, chopped finely
- 2 cups Arborio rice
- 1½ cups asparagus, tough ends removed and cut into 1-inch chunks
- 1 cup cherry tomatoes
- 3 garlic cloves, minced
- 3 cups low-sodium chicken broth
- 2 tablespoons fresh lemon juice
- 1 teaspoon dried oregano
- Salt, to taste
- 2/3 cup Parmesan cheese, shredded

Method:

1. Place the butter in the Instant Pot and select "Sauté". Then add the onions and cook for about 3 minutes.
2. Add the rice and stir fry for about 3 minutes.
3. Select the "Cancel" and stir in the veggies, broth, lemon juice, oregano and salt.
4. Secure the lid and place the pressure valve to "Seal" position.
5. Select "Manual" and cook under "High Pressure" for about 6 minutes. Select the "Cancel" and carefully do a "Quick" release.
6. Remove the lid and stir in the Parmesan cheese.
7. Serve warm.

Meal Prep Tip: Transfer the risotto into a large bowl and keep aside to cool completely. Divide the risotto into 8 plastic bags. Seal the bags and refrigerate for up to 2-3 days. Just before serving, in a pan boil a little bit of the broth and stir in the risotto. Cook until heated through. Stir in the Parmesan and serve.

Nutritional Value per Serving:

- *Calories 267*
- *Fiber 2.8 g*
- *Sugar 2.4 g*
- *Protein 8.9 g*

Veggie Pilaf

Preparation Time: 15 minutes

Cooking Time: 10 minutes

Servings: 8

Ingredients:

- 1 tablespoon butter
- 1 medium onion, chopped
- 1 celery stalk, chopped
- 1 large carrot, chopped
- 2 cups long grain white rice, rinsed
- 14-ounce vegetable broth
- 1¼ cups water
- Salt, to taste
- 1 cup frozen peas, thawed
- 2 tablespoons fresh parsley, chopped
- ½ cup almonds, toasted and sliced

Method:

1. Place the butter in the Instant Pot and select "Sauté". Then add the onion, celery and carrot and cook for about 4-5 minutes.
2. Stir in the rice and cook for about 1-2 minutes.
3. Select the "Cancel" and stir in the broth, water and salt.
4. Secure the lid and place the pressure valve to "Seal" position.
5. Select "Manual" and cook under "High Pressure" for about 3 minutes.
6. Select the "Cancel" and carefully do a "Natural" release for about 5 minutes and then do a "Quick" release.
7. Remove the lid and with a fork, fluff the rice.
8. Stir in the peas, parsley and almonds, and serve immediately.

Meal Prep Tip: Transfer the pilaf into a large bowl and keep aside to cool completely. Divide the pilaf into 8 containers evenly. Cover the containers and refrigerate for up to 1-2 days. Just before serving, drizzle a teaspoon of water over the top of rice and reheat in the microwave.

Nutritional Value per Serving:

- Calories 249
- Total Fat 5.1 g
- Saturated Fat 1.3 g
- Cholesterol 4 mg

- Sodium 213 mg
- Total Carbs 43.6 g
- Fiber 3 g
- Sugar 2.4 g
- Protein 6.9 g
- Potassium 221 mg

Chili Mac n Cheese

Preparation Time: 15 minutes

Cooking Time: 4 minutes

Servings: 6

Ingredients:

- 2 (14-ounce) cans spicy chili
- 1 (12-ounce) can beer
- ½ cup water
- 2 cups elbow macaroni
- ½ cup cashew milk

Method:

1. In the pot of Instant Pot, place all the ingredients except the milk and stir to combine.
2. Secure the lid and place the pressure valve to "Seal" position.
3. Select "Manual" and cook under "High Pressure" for about 4 minutes.
4. Select the "Cancel" and carefully do a "Quick" release.
5. Remove the lid and stir in cashew milk.
6. Serve immediately.

Meal Prep Tip: Transfer the mac n cheese into a large bowl and keep aside to cool completely. Divide the mac n cheese into 6 containers evenly. Cover the containers and refrigerate for up to 1-2 days. Just before serving, drizzle with a little milk and reheat in the microwave.

Nutritional Value per Serving:

- *Calories 310*
- *Total Fat 6.4 g*
- *Saturated Fat 0.8 g*
- *Cholesterol 0 mg*
- *Sodium 452 mg*
- *Total Carbs 45.3 g*
- *Fiber 5.5 g*
- *Sugar 3.9 g*
- *Protein 13.5 g*
- *Potassium 94 mg*

CHAPTER 13: DESSERT RECIPES

Rice Pudding

Preparation Time: 10 minutes
Cooking Time: 20 minutes
Servings: 6
Ingredients:

- 5 cups unsweetened almond milk
- ½ cup medium-grain white rice
- ½ cup sugar
- 3 tablespoons cashews, chopped
- 3 tablespoons almonds, chopped
- 1 teaspoon ground cardamom

Method:

1. In the pot of Instant Pot, mix together all ingredients.
2. Secure the lid and place the pressure valve to "Seal" position.
3. Select "Manual" and cook under "High Pressure" for about 20 minutes.
4. Select the "Cancel" and carefully do a Natural release.
5. Remove the lid and transfer the pudding into serving bowls.
6. Keep aside to cool slightly.
7. Top with nuts and serve warm.

Meal Prep Tip: Transfer the pudding into a large bowl and keep aside to cool completely. Divide the pudding into 6 containers evenly. Cover the containers and refrigerate for up to 1-2 days. Serve chilled or reheat in the microwave slightly.

Nutritional Value per Serving:

- *Calories 195*
- *Total Fat 6.5 g*
- *Saturated Fat 0.8 g*
- *Cholesterol 0 mg*
- *Sodium 152 mg*
- *Total Carbs 33 g*
- *Fiber 1.6 g*
- *Sugar 17 g*
- *Protein 3.3 g*
- *Potassium 226 mg*

Pumpkin Pudding

Preparation Time: 10 minutes

Cooking Time: 30 minutes

Servings: 6

Ingredients:

- ½ cup coconut milk
- 2 teaspoons gelatin
- ¾ cup canned pumpkin puree, drained well
- 1 egg
- ½ cup coconut sugar
- 1 teaspoon ground cinnamon
- ½ teaspoon ground allspice
- ½ teaspoon ground ginger
- ½ teaspoon ground nutmeg
- ¼ teaspoon ground cloves
- ¼ teaspoon salt
- 1 cup water

Method:

1. In a pan, add milk and sprinkle with gelatin.
2. Place pan over medium-low heat and cook until milk is just heated through, beating continuously.
3. Remove from heat and keep aside.
4. In a bowl, add gelatin mixture, pumpkin, egg, coconut sugar, spices and salt and beat until smooth.
5. Transfer mixture into greased soufflé dish.
6. Arrange a steamer trivet in the bottom of Instant Pot and pour 1 cup of water.
7. Arrange the soufflé dish on top of trivet.
8. Secure the lid and place the pressure valve to "Seal" position.
9. Select "Manual" and cook under "High Pressure" for about 30 minutes.
10. Select the "Cancel" and carefully do a "Quick" release.
11. Remove the lid and transfer the soufflé dish onto a wire rack to cool completely.
12. Refrigerator for about 4-6 hours before serving.

Meal Prep Tip: Transfer the pudding into a large bowl and keep aside to cool completely. Divide the pudding into 6 containers evenly. Cover the containers and refrigerate for up to 1-2 days. Serve chilled.

Nutritional Value per Serving:

- Calories 116
- Total Fat 5.7 g
- Saturated Fat 4.6 g
- Cholesterol 27 mg
- Sodium 117 mg
- Total Carbs 16.3 g
- Fiber 1.7 g
- Sugar 13.8 g
- Protein 3.2 g
- Potassium 253 mg

Egg Custard

Preparation Time: 15 minutes

Cooking Time: 6 minutes

Servings: 4

Ingredients:

- 8 large egg yolks
- 1/3 cup granulated sugar
- 1 teaspoon vanilla extract
- Pinch of salt
- 2 cups cream
- 1 teaspoon ground cinnamon

Method:

1. In a large bowl, add the egg yolks, granulated sugar, vanilla and salt and beat until well combined.
2. Add the cream and beat until well combined.
3. With a strainer, strain the mixture, stirring continuously.
4. Transfer the mixture into 4 large ramekins.
5. With foil pieces, cover the ramekins.
6. In the bottom of Instant Pot, arrange a steamer trivet and pour 1½ cups of water.
7. Place the ramekins on top of trivet.
8. Secure the lid and place the pressure valve to "Seal" position.
9. Select "Manual" and cook under "High Pressure" for about 6 minutes.
10. Select the "Cancel" and carefully do a "Quick" release.
11. Remove the lid and transfer the ramekins onto a wire rack.
12. Remove the foil pieces and let them cool slightly.
13. With plastic wrap, cover the ramekins and refrigerate to chill for at least 3-4 hours.
14. Sprinkle with cinnamon before serving.

Meal Prep Tip: Remove the ramekins from Instant Pot and immediately, place in ice bath to cool completely. With plastic wraps, cover each ramekin and for up to 1-2 days. Serve chilled.

Nutritional Value per Serving:

- *Calories 252*
- *Cholesterol 442 mg*
- *Total Carbs 22.2 g*
- *Sugar 19.4 g*
- *Protein 6.4 g*

Sweet Potato Halwa

Preparation Time: 15 minutes

Cooking Time: 6 minutes

Servings: 4

Ingredients:

- 2 tablespoons ghee
- 3 medium sweet potatoes, peeled and sliced thinly
- ¼ cup unsweetened almond milk
- 1/3 cup packed brown sugar
- ¼ cup grated unsweetened coconut
- ½ teaspoon salt
- 6-8 green cardamom pods
- Pinch of saffron threads, crumbled
- 2 tablespoon pistachio slices

Method:

1. Place the ghee in the Instant Pot and select "Sauté". Then add the sweet potato slices and cook for about 2-3 minutes.
2. Select the "Cancel" and stir in the remaining ingredients except pistachio slices.
3. Secure the lid and place the pressure valve to "Seal" position.
4. Select "Manual" and cook under "High Pressure" for about 3 minutes.
5. Select the "Cancel" and carefully do a "Natural" release.
6. Remove the lid and serve warm with the garnishing of pistachio slices.

Meal Prep Tip: Transfer the halwa into a large bowl and keep aside to cool completely. Divide the halwa into 4 containers evenly. Cover the containers and refrigerate for up to 1-2 days. Reheat in the microwave slightly before serving.

Nutritional Value per Serving:

- *Calories 265*
- *Total Fat 9.3 g*
- *Saturated Fat 5.6 g*
- *Cholesterol 16 mg*
- *Sodium 327 mg*
- *Total Carbs 44.6 g*
- *Fiber 5.3 g*
- *Protein 2.4 g*
- *Potassium 984 mg*

Apple Crisp

Preparation Time: 15 minutes

Cooking Time: 8 minutes

Servings: 6

Ingredients:

- ¾ cup old fashioned rolled oats
- ¼ cup flour
- 4 tablespoons butter, melted
- ¼ cup brown sugar
- ¼ teaspoon salt
- 5 medium apples, peeled, cored and cut into chunks
- 2 teaspoons ground cinnamon
- ½ teaspoon ground nutmeg
- ½ cup water
- 1 tablespoon honey

Method:

1. In a bowl, add oats, flour, butter, brown sugar and salt and mix well.
2. In the bottom of Instant Pot, place apple chunks and sprinkle with cinnamon and nutmeg.
3. Top with water and honey.
4. With spoonful, drop oats mixture on top of the apples.
5. Secure the lid and place the pressure valve to "Seal" position.
6. Select "Manual" and cook under "High Pressure" for about 8 minutes.
7. Select the "Cancel" and carefully do a Natural release.
8. Remove the lid and serve warm.

Meal Prep Tip: Remove the crisp from Instant Pot and transfer into a heatproof bowl. Immediately, place the bowl in ice bath to cool completely. Transfer the crisp into containers and freeze for unto 3-4 months. On serving day, thaw the crisp in refrigerator for about 2 hours. Place in the oven at 350 degrees uncovered for about 20 minutes.

Nutritional Value per Serving:

- Calories 257
- Total Fat 8.8 g
- Saturated Fat 5 g
- Cholesterol 20 mg
- Fiber 6.1 g
- Protein 2.5 g

Carrot Fudge

Preparation Time: 15 minutes

Cooking Time: 18 minutes

Servings: 12

Ingredients:

- 3 tablespoon ghee
- 4 cups carrots, peeled and grated
- 4 tablespoons cashews, chopped and divided
- 4 tablespoons almonds, chopped and divided
- ¾ cup warm milk
- ½ cup sugar
- ½ cup almond flour
- ½ cup nonfat milk powder
- ½ teaspoon ground cardamom

Method:

1. Place the ghee in the Instant Pot and select "Sauté". Then add the carrots and half of each cashews and almonds and sauté for about 2-3 minutes.
2. Select the "Cancel" and stir in warm milk and sugar.
3. Secure the lid and place the pressure valve to "Seal" position.
4. Select "Manual" and cook under "High Pressure" for about 5 minutes.
5. Select the "Cancel" and carefully do a "Quick" release.
6. Remove the lid and select "Sauté".
7. Stir in almond flour and milk powder and cook for about 8-10 minutes, stirring frequently.
8. Stir in cardamom and select the "Cancel".
9. Transfer the carrot mixture into a parchment lined baking dish evenly and with the back of a spoon, smooth the top.
10. Sprinkle with remaining cashews and almonds and gently press into the fudge.
11. Refrigerate, covered for about 30-60 minute.
12. Remove from refrigerator and cut into desired sized squares.

Meal Prep Tip: Wrap these squares in waxed paper and preserve in refrigerator by placing in an airtight container.

Nutritional Value per Serving:

- *Calories 140*
- *Total Fat 8.2 g*
- *Saturated Fat 2.7 g*

- *Cholesterol 10 mg*
- *Sodium 38 mg*
- *Total Carbs 15.6 g*
- *Fiber 1.8 g*
- *Sugar 11.7 g*
- *Protein 3 g*
- *Potassium 174 mg*

Pumpkin Muffins

Preparation Time: 15 minutes

Cooking Time: 7 minutes

Servings: 18

Ingredients:

For Muffins:

- 7/8 cup all-purpose flour
- ¾ teaspoon baking powder
- 1/8 teaspoon baking soda
- ¼ teaspoon ground allspice
- ¼ teaspoon ground cinnamon
- 1/8 teaspoon salt
- ¾ cup white sugar
- ¼ cup butter, softened
- 4-ounce canned pumpkin puree
- 1 egg
- 1 egg white
- 2 tablespoons yogurt
- ¼ teaspoon vanilla extract

For Filling:

- 8-ounce cream cheese, softened
- ¼ cup sugar
- 2 tablespoons yogurt
- ½ teaspoon orange peel, grated
- ¼ teaspoon vanilla extract
- 1 egg
- 1 egg yolk

Method:

1. For muffins: in a bowl, mix together flour, baking powder, baking soda, spices and salt.
2. In another bowl, add sugar and butter and beat until fluffy.
3. Add pumpkin puree, egg, egg white, yogurt and vanilla extract and gently, mix until just combined.
4. Add flour mixture into egg mixture and mix until just combined.
5. Add about 1½ tablespoons of mixture into each of 18 mini silicon muffin cups.
6. For filling: in a bowl, add cream cheese, sugar, yogurt, orange peel and vanilla extract and beat until smooth.

7. Add egg and egg yolk and mix until just combined.
8. Add filling into a pastry bag and pipe deep in the center of each muffin mixture.
9. In the bottom of Instant Pot, arrange a steamer basket and pour 1½ cups of water.
10. Place half of muffin cups on top of trivet and cover with a piece of foil.
11. Arrange a second trivet on top.
12. Place remaining muffin cups on top of trivet and cover with a piece of foil.
13. Secure the lid and place the pressure valve to "Seal" position.
14. Select "Manual" and cook under "High Pressure" for about 7 minutes.
15. Select the "Cancel" and carefully do a "Natural" release for about 15 minutes and then do a "Quick" release.
16. Remove the lid and transfer the muffin cups onto a wire rack.
17. Remove the foil pieces and cool for about 10 minutes before serving.

Meal Prep Tip: Carefully invert the muffins onto a wire rack to cool completely. Line 1-2 airtight container with paper towels. Arrange muffins over paper towel in a single layer. Cover muffins with another paper towel. Refrigerate for about 2-3 days. Reheat in the microwave on High for about 2 minutes before serving.

Nutritional Value per Serving:
- Calories 147
- Total Fat 7.8 g
- Saturated Fat 4.7 g
- Cholesterol 51 mg
- Sodium 91 mg
- Total Carbs 17.1 g
- Fiber 0.4 g
- Sugar 11.7 g
- Protein 2.8 g
- Potassium 76 mg

Lime Pie

Preparation Time: 15 minutes

Cooking Time: 22 minutes

Servings: 8

Ingredients:

For Crust:

- ¾ cup graham cracker crumbs
- 3 tablespoons unsalted butter, melted
- 1 tablespoon sugar

For Filling:

- 1 (14-ounce) can sweetened condensed milk
- 4 large egg yolks
- ½ cup fresh key lime juice
- 1/3 cup sour cream
- 2 tablespoons key lime zest, grated

Method:

1. Grease a 7-inch springform pan.
2. For crust: in a small bowl, add all ingredients and mix until well combined.
3. Place mixture into prepared pan and press evenly in the bottom and up the side of the pan. Freeze for about 10 minutes.
4. For filling: in a large bowl, add egg yolks and beat until light yellow.
5. Slowly, add sweetened condensed milk and bat until mixture becomes thick.
6. Slowly, add lime juice and beat until smooth.
7. Stir in sour cream and lime zest.
8. Place filing mixture over crust evenly. With a piece of foil, cover top of spring form pan.
9. In the bottom of Instant Pot, arrange a steamer trivet and pour 1 cup of water.
10. Place the springform pan on top of trivet.
11. Secure the lid and place the pressure valve to "Seal" position.
12. Select "Manual" and cook under "High Pressure" for about 15 minutes.
13. Select the "Cancel" and carefully do a "Natural" release for about 10 minutes and then do a "Quick" release.
14. Remove the lid and transfer the springform pan onto a wire rack.
15. Remove the foil piece and cool completely.
16. With a plastic wrap, over the pan and refrigerate for at least 4 hours before serving.

Meal Prep Tip: Wrap the pie tightly in a few layers of plastic wrap and then place in a large resealable bag. Seal the bag and refrigerate for about 4 days. On serving day, place in the oven at 375 degrees for about 15 minutes.

Nutritional Value per Serving:

- Calories 289
- Total Fat 13.7 g
- Saturated Fat 7.5 g
- Cholesterol 137 mg
- Sodium 173 mg
- Total Carbs 36.3 g
- Fiber 0.7 g
- Sugar 30.1 g
- Protein 6.1 g
- Potassium 211 mg

CONCLUSION

Meal prepping is the process of preparing food for a certain amount of days or even a week beforehand. It requires meal planning which is devising a proper and thorough plan for preparing the food and then drafting a shopping list involving all the ingredients involved in the plan for prepping. There are many benefits of meal prepping which ranges from financial to health benefits and the top most is the time saving factor which makes it attractive the most. Before meal prepping do proper research about your meal planning and don't opt for complicated meals in the beginning. Have proper containers for meal storage and don't cook too much of a single recipe. Keep your menu plans versatile and nutritious for better health and taste. The most important thing is the Instant Pot, it lets you cook all your food in a short time span, without effecting the nutrients.

95329130R00064